Alpine Flowers and Gardens

G. Flemwell

DODO PRESS

ALPINE FLOWERS AND GARDENS

PAINTED AND DESCRIBED BY G. FLEMWELL

1909

TO MY MOTHER.

Alpine Garden (La Linnea) At Bourg St. Pierre, In August.

CONTENTS

PREFACE

'Un volume sur la flore alpine, dira-t-on, il en existe beaucoup déjà, et il y a, dans ce domaine, surproduction. Eh bien, oui, il en existe beaucoup, mais je ne connais rien qui s'approche du travail que Mr. Flemwell a bien voulu me demander de présenter au public. II s'agit içi, non d'un ouvrage de botanique simplement, mais d'un poëme, d'un chant à la louange de la nature alpine et alpestre et ce chant est l'ceuvre d'un artiste que le public jugera par son oeuvre et qui, à mon avis, a compris la vraie nature de la montagne. Sous l'angle où elle nous est présentée, la flore alpine n'a encore jamais été décrite ni offerte au public. II y a donc içi une oeuvre profondément originale, à laquelle les amateurs du Beau et du Vrai ne pourront qu'applaudir.

La flore alpine est plus populaire qu'elle ne l'a jamais été. A mesure que l'amour des courses de montagne se développe, le besoin de connaître la flore des hauteurs augmente aussi. La vivacité des coloris, la beauté des formes, tout a été donné en partage à cette végétation si spéciale qui orne les pâturages, les rochers, les éboulis de nos vieilles Alpes. Ajoutez à cela l'originalité du port des plantes, cette compression des formes qui raccourcit et supprime parfois les tiges, la grandeur des corolles relativement au feuillage et vous comprendrez qu'on puisse s'enthousiasmer pour la flore des Alpes.

Cet enthousiasme va si loin que le passant qui admire, voudrait jouir plus longtemps et conserver la vue de ces beautés, l'emporter chez lui. On arrache quelques pieds des espèces les plus apparentes et l'on essaie de les acclimater chez soi sans y réussir toujours. C'est que, pour ce faire, il importe de procéder avec méthode, de suivre les conseils des practiciens, par exemple d'arracher les plantes alors qu'elles sont à l'état de repos, après leur floraison. Le meilleur procédé est, d'ailleurs, celui du semis et c'est aussi le plus aisé à pratiquer.

On a, depuis une vingtaine d'années, établi dans toutes nos montagnes, mais plus spécialement dans la chaîne alpine, des jardins alpins dans les régions mêmes où croissent les plantes alpines. Ces jardins, vrais musées vivants où l'on rassemble les plantes les plus belles et les plus intéressantes pour les mettre à la portée du public, sont aussi des écoles à la disposition des touristes qui passent ou des étudiants qui ont à étudier la biologie, la systématique ou toute autre question botanique. Ils sont situés généralement dans des lieux très accessibles, sont ouverts au public et contribuent pour une bonne part à cultiver l'amour pour la flore des montagnes. Dans la plupart de ces jardins on cultive les plantes de toutes les régions montagneuses du globe et l'on réunit, dans un cadre plus ou moins restreint, les espèces caractéristiques des Alpes, du Jura, des Pyrénées, Carpathes, Apennins, Balcans, du Caucase, de l'Himalaya, de la Sibérie, de la Chine, du Japon, des Cordillères américaines, des montagnes de l'Afrique centrale, de la Nouvelk Zélande, des régions arctiques et antarctiques, boréales et hyperboréales.

On comprend dès lors l'intérêt qu'offrent ces cultures, car, par elles, on peut se rendre compte de la similitude des flores de toutes les montagnes du monde, ce qui permet d'établir que: à des conditions semblables d'existence correspond une végétation semblable dans son aspect et sa nature. Mais, cela nous a permis aussi de constater la supériorité incontestable de notre flore alpine et européenne au point de vue de l'éclat des couleurs sur celles de presque toutes les autres montagnes, l'Himalaya excepté.

Le volume de M. Flemwell arrive donc à point pour nous en faire connaître le côté esthétique et artistique et, en ma qualité de Suisse et de vieil alpiniste qui a parcouru la chaîne alpine d'un bout à l'autre, je tiens à le remercier pour le monument qu'il vient d'élever à la flore de mon pays.

Henry Correvon

Geneva, November, 1909.

CHAPTER I. THE RIVAL SEASONS

Switzerland probably owes nearly as much of its popularity to its flowers as it does to its mountains, and although in this regard we may find it difficult to dissociate the one from the other, it is not impossible, nor, indeed, unreasonable. There is a season when the mountains are devoid of flowers and yet remain popular. But the popularity which surrounds the Alps in winter is not, and probably never can be, the wide popularity which surrounds them in spring, summer, and early autumn. Whilst Goddess Flora slumbers, Nature's appeal is more particular than general, and this even to so strenuous, athletic, and sports-loving a race as the British; for, as Mr. E. T. Cook so rightly remarks in the opening chapter of his 'Gar ens of England,' 'there is a love of flowers fast knit into the very fibre of our British nature.' Rocks and crags radiant with gem-like florets must exercise a fascination far more universal than when brown and bare - a fascination which must reach even most climbers climbing for mere climbing's sake. The Matterhorn or the Jungfrau, set amid a glory of Rhododendron and Gentian, must ever have more constant admirers than when wrapped about with snow. Slopes dyed richly with red and blue and gold must ever make wider appeal than when draped merely in white. For white, in human economy, is a luxury - a wholesome condition for a select season. It soon has palled upon the imagination; it soon has served its useful purpose of duly stimulating appreciation for an estate more sentient, more colourfull, and - yes, more vital.

'The winter Alps are melancholy,' says Leslie Stephen in 'The Playground of Europe,' 'as everything sublime is more or less melancholy;' and it is just this melancholy - 'this living death, or cataleptic trance of the mountains' - which, fascinating though it be for awhile, soon palls. Or, at any rate, its effect is this upon the generality of mankind. The generality of mankind are not Leslie Stephens. The generality of mankind, I venture to think, could not write a long book about the Alps, as he has done, without mentioning the unique and wondrous flora more than to remark: 'It is pleasant to lie on one's back in a bed of Rhododendrons and look up to a mountain - top peering at one from above a bank of cloud.'

It is true, quite true, that 'the Alps in winter belong to dreamland.' It is true, quite true, that 'from the moment when the traveller catches sight, from the terraces of the Jura, of the long escarpment of peaks from Mont Blanc to the Wetter-horn to the time when he has penetrated to the innermost recesses of the chain, he is passing through a series of dreams within dreams. Each vision is a portal to one beyond and within, still more substantial and solemn. One passes by slow gradations to the more and more shadowy regions, where the stream of life runs lower, and the enchantment binds the senses with a more powerful opiate.' All this is true, quite true. But 'there are dreams and dreams,' as Sir Leslie himself elsewhere says; and I make so bold as to think that the dreams engendered by these selfsame Alps in a setting of floral wonders must ever obtain a larger, more real, and even healthier hold upon the imagination and enthusiasm of humanity.

Our most insistent demand is for something more in tune with the human joie de vivre - for some more intimate touch of Nature which will make all things akin. And this, assuredly, the flowers contribute to the otherwise superb melancholy of the Alps.

I know of no more dream-like and inspiring sight than when, in early spring-time, the mystic Alps, ridding themselves of their superfluous snows, are thundering down avalanches over their mighty crags and cliffs, and yet the while, in the tranquil, grassy foreground lies a lovely new-born wealth of Soldanella. Here at once is the melancholy, mystic grandeur of winter healthily allied with the more intimate interest of living colour, making of the whole an experience whose appeal is, and must be, far more irresistible and general than if winter stood alone, mistress of the entire landscape.

'One cannot be, and ought not to be, for ever on the snow.' This is the opinion of that veteran Alpinist and lover of the Alps, Mr. Frederick Harrison, in speaking of 'the superstition that glaciers and snow-peaks are the only things in the Alps worth coming to see.' He dubs it 'a silly conceit'; and so, undoubtedly, it is. Let it be repeated: whiteness for man is a luxury. Among his main and necessary elements of sustenance is colour, pronounced and varied. Whatever his spirit may yearn for in snow, 'the body's coloured pride' will not be gainsaid; its clamour is loud and imperative. Steely-blue has been the prevailing colour throughout the winter - a colour which, whatever the fascination of its appeal, can never be the same full, intimate appeal of the blue-blue of the Gentian. It is, therefore, with very real and reasonable enthusiasm that men wait upon the reawakening of their goddess; and it is with enthusiasm equally real and reasonable that they should give to Alpine flowers their due - a prominent place among the popularity-compelling beauties of the Alps.

Now, many observers affect to believe that this popularity is waning, and that the Swiss Alps have seen their best days as an attraction to the student and lover of Nature. I find it difficult to subscribe to this. It does not seem to me to be true even for the seeker after 'new sensations.' Quite the contrary: I find considerably more justification for believing that the popularity of the Alps has as yet by no means reached its zenith. Compared with the vast army of tourists and others annually visiting Switzerland, it is but the few who know its Alps in some of their most bewitching and distinctive moments. Comparatively few are in the mountains in early spring, or, indeed, know the mountains during any part of spring. About the middle or end of February there is a rush away from the mountains, away from the threatened melting of the snow; and the return thither, in any marked degree, is not until late in June or early in July. And during the interval - during, that is to say, the months of April and May - there is in progress a rapid and delightful transformation which it were a thousand pities to miss: a transformation such as no other months can supply.

As the snow recedes, the brown bed of the pine-forests is decked with myriads of Hepatica; their thick clusters of mauve-blue blossoms, relieved here and there by the rarer forms of white and rose, glint gaily among the sombre tree-trunks, creating a veritable laughing fairyland where, usually, all is sedate, if not actually gloomy. The gorges are peopled with the nodding caps, tipped green and yellow, of the large Snowflake (Leucojum vernum), and with the white, brush-like heads of the Butterbur (Petasites niveus), while the damp and rocky sides of these gorges are stained magenta-red by innumerable tufts of the Sticky Primrose (Primula viscosa) nestling in every nook and cranny. Over the plateaux, as far as eye can roam, spreads a silvery haze of white and purple as the Crocus and the Soldanella are freed from their winter covering; on every hand, upon sunny bank and grassy slope, blue is strewn in dazzling profusion - that pure and matchless blue of the little Vernal Gentian - sometimes to be happily intermingled with the pale yellow of Liottard's Star of Bethlehem (Gagea Liottardi), or with the brilliant gold of Geum and Potentilla; while the more marshy ground, acre upon acre, lies rose-red and brazen with its densely packed burden of Primula farinosa, the Mealy, or Bird's-eye Primrose, and with the Marsh Marigold.

All of this, and much more, is missed by the majority of visitors, who arrive perhaps in time to see the last fast-fading blossoms of the Rhododendron. Of course, they do find vestiges of spring's abundance, but only vestiges. From the very nature of the Alps, spring lingers long upon them, and often may be found nestling side by side with summer. On the ground higher up than it is necessary to go in the earlier months, on some sequestered slope, or in some shaded hollow where the snow has taken a tardy departure, or where, even, it may still be lingering, these summer visitors will frequently come upon bright patches of the earlier spring flowers. But it is nothing compared with what has gone before - nothing compared with the sumptuous feast which has earlier been spread, to right and to left, on the lower sun-favoured ground. What they find, however, is an inspiring and suggestive sample of a wealth which mere words utterly fail to picture properly. Of tales of this wealth they will hear; their appetites will be whetted for the feast; and surely will they make mental resolve to encompass, another year, this marvellous and distinctive season.

Because, then, the possibilities of the Alps are not as yet known or appreciated as they should be and, assuredly, as they will be, it seems safe to say that they have by no means reached the zenith of their popularity. Already, indeed, one can remark a development in this direction. Already many mountain hotels and pensions make arrangements to meet an earlier demand upon their hospitality, Already, quite early in May, British and other wayfarers may be found delightedly established in many an 'out-o'-way' place, indulging in day-long rapture over the wonders so lavishly unfolded April before them by the increasing year. For, just in the same way as they have found out and recognized of late the healthiness and fascination of Alpland in winter, so are they coming to see that spring has its possibilities equally great, if not, indeed, greater.

Hepatica In The Woods At Bex, In The Rhone Valley.

CHAPTER II. SPRING IN THE ALPS

If comparisons are often odious, it is because they often serve to very small purpose, and often lead to much injustice. Prejudice usually plays a conspicuous part in them; predilections already exist, and our comparisons are thus rendered markedly unscientific. In nothing is this more true than in attempting comparison between spring in the Swiss Alps and spring in England. The Englishman will vaunt his spring to you as something incomparable. Well, he is right in a sense. Let him leave it at that: it is incomparable. It is incomparable just as the Alpine spring is incomparable. Conditions are so different that it is useless and unjust to go into comparisons with any idea of putting one above the other in the end. Each is best in its way; each is unique; each is fascinating and wholly delightful. As well say that a cat is wrong because it does not wag its tail with pleasure like a dog as say that an English spring stands first and foremost because it is more balmy, homely, and reposeful than an Alpine spring. A cat does not rank lower than a dog because the waving of its tail is less homely and reposeful than the wagging of a dog's tail. It is of small use, and it leads to great injustice, to conduct comparison upon such lines as these. Both the dog and the cat stand equally right in the use of their tails; and both the English spring and the Alpine spring are equally lovely, though cast in somewhat different moulds.

No; it is best not to attempt comparison. Let us study differences if we will, but leave comparisons alone. What has been called 'the quiet bandbox scenery of cultivated England' lends itself to a very distinctive exposition of spring-time delights. Scenes such as depicted with so much truth and humour by W. H. Drummond, the poet of the Canadian Habitants; scenes such as ' W'en small sheep is firs' comin' out on de pasture, Deir nice leetle tail stickin' up on deir back, Dey ronne wit' deir moder, an' play wit' each oder. An' jomp all de tam jus' de sam' dey was crack!

'An' ole cow also, she's glad winter is over, So she kick herse'f up, an' start off on de race Wit' de two-year-ole heifer, dat's purty soon lef' her - W'y ev'ryt'ings crazee all over de place.'

Scenes such as these, though they be of the very essence of spring in England, are altogether foreign to spring in the Swiss Alps. So also are the rookeries and rabbit-warrens, the hedgerows of hawthorn, the banks of primroses, the nut-woods carpeted with bluebells, the copses gay with foxgloves - and much besides. In fact, the whole 'atmosphere' differs, for the larger part of the fundamentals of an English spring are absent in the spring of the Alps. And yet the Alps have a spring no whit less entrancing than the spring of England.

In the Alps the steel-blue of winter is still in the air - indeed, one feels it in the very flowers. Even though no snowy Alp be in sight, and nothing but floral gaiety around, there is yet a sense of austerity. The vegetation, though colourfull, is neither coarse nor rank, nor even luxurious, as judged by English standard. Nature is crisp and brisk; the air is thin and clear; everywhere is great refinement - yes, refinement; that, perhaps, is the better word - refinement quite other than that of spring in England. It were as though the severity of the struggle for existence could be read in the sweet face of things, just as we may often read it in the smiling face of some chastened human being lines of sweetness running side by side with lines of acute capacity; a strong face beautiful; a face in which optimism reigns sovereign over an active pessimism. Nature in the Alps is instinct with the stern necessity for perpetual endeavour, whereas in England, where conditions are not so harsh, we have a sense of a certain indolence and ease of circumstance of Nature which we call homeliness and repose. Repose, in this sense, there certainly is not in the Alpine spring. Every suspicion of lassitude or laissez-faire is unknown; all is keen and buoyant, quick with an earnest joie de vivre which is as exquisite in its way as anything more voluptuously sentimental that England can produce We feel small want to loll about and dream; the one impulse is to be up and exploring the wonders to be found on every side, and to do the while our dreaming, Not that these wonders are new to us, and therefore incentive to energy; we may know them all well of old, but the infection is the same. Spring in the Alps is redolent of energy. The cattle, goats, and sheep, are not yet here for us to watch the romping of. We it is, young and old, who do the skipping!

And this energy is felt the moment the hem of Alpine altitudes is touched; we are instantly inspired by that refinement already alluded to. Maybe we shall have to walk for an hour, or perhaps more, from our hotel before reaching really representative Alpine vegetation. It will be the case at such mountain resorts as, for instance, Chateau-d'Cex, Villars-sur-Ollon, or Finhaut; for it is not everywhere, as at Champex or at the Col de la Forclaz, that true Alpine abundance is to be found at our very door. Up through a belt of forest we must often wend our way ere we reach our quest. And here it is that some small fatigue may possibly be felt, for the paths are steep and 'rough and ready,' and there is little of the particular interest of which we are in search. Stopping to gather breath, we shall perhaps exclaim: 'Where are these wonderful pastures of which we have heard so much? Where is this fairyland? Pines, nothing but pines, seem to be ahead!' Patience! presently we shall have forgotten this little toil; for we shall suddenly emerge from the forest into the open - into the Promised Land of Plenty.

The path steepens for awhile, and presently sharply rounds a great wall of rock; and then, before we are well aware of what has happened, the curtain has lifted, the sombre forest is behind us, and we are face to face with one of the most perfect of Alpine landscapes imaginable. From where we are standing, a glory of colour, broken here and there by great grey boulders and the dark, rich foliage of Rhododendron-bushes, stretches up and away until it dies in a haze of lively tints against the slopes and rugged cliffs of a stately snow-clad Alp. The transition has been so unexpectedly sudden as to surprise all utterance, and it is some time before we can realize our feelings. Rumour and report have not exaggerated; they have not even done justice to the scene. All fatigue has fled; energy is in the air, and pervades everything. We are indeed in fairyland!

The feast opens with gentle slope rising above slope, clothed with close, moss-like grass of a brilliance such as only the Alps can produce, and strewn with a profusion of Bell-Gentian, known casually as Gentiana acavlis, but strictly as G. Kocldana or G. eoccisa, in all its varying shades, from rich French-blue to dark blue-purple; while, waving gently in the stirring air over this dazzling carpet of blue and green, are hosts of the large and lovely white Anemone (Anemone alpina), happy hunting-ground of 'the irreverent, buccaneering bee,' working already with all his proverbial busyness. Some butterflies, too, have made their appearance. For the most part, they are Tyndarus, Phyrrha, and Pasiphce, Alpine members of the family of 'Browns' - a family, as most collectors know, of special complexity and interest, in spite of its usually demure colouring.

Following the path as it winds up these wonderfully dressed slopes, and passing several drier mounds covered with the varying forms of that fascinating little 'everlasting' known popularly as Mountain Cudweed and botanically as Anten-naria dioica, we come to some hollows where snow is still sparsely lying. Here the ground is yet brown, but already it is sown with a wealth of the sky-blue Gentian (Gentiana verna), interspersed with many a curiously silky tuft of the purple Windflower (Anemone vernalis). Close at hand are broad patches of Soldanella (Soldanella alpina), associating with crowds of Crocus vernus and with many a specimen of Ranunculus pyrenceus, the dainty white Pyrenean Crowfoot of such fragile, fleeting flower; while, on some soft but stony ground near by, we have innumerable moss-like tufts of that little white, yellow-eyed gem, Andro-sace Chamcejasme.

Crocus And Soldanella At Les Plans, With The Mountains Of Savoy In The Background. April.

Wending our way slowly - for hurry were un seemly, if not impossible, amid such surroundings - we arrive at a stretch of flatter ground, marshy, and intersected by several shallow streamlets. Here is a wealth of Primula farinosa, its fresh, rosy hue enhanced by the dark purple-brown of Bartsia alpina, lavishly mingled with the bright blue stars of that tiniest of Gentians, Qentiana nivalis, while standing over this sea of pink and blue are regiments of the clear yellow Trollius europceus, or Globe-flower. Nestling on the spongy Sphagnum moss are colonies of Sundew (Drosera rotundifolid) and Butterwort (Pinguicula vulgaris), among which creeps the tiny, fragile Vaccinium oxycoccus, with small pink blossoms, whose petals, turned back, give it something of the appearance of a diminutive Cyclamen.

Continuing our way, the nature of the ground once more alters, and we come to steep and verdant sun-bathed slopes ascending to the cliffs and snows of the mighty peak above. And although the details of the scene may change, the seemingly unending panorama of varied colour continues. Here the many-flowered, apple-blossom-tinted heads of Anemone narcissiflora replace the large white flowers of Anemone alpina, and the carpet from which they are springing, though still retaining a profusion of Bell-Gentian, consists mainly of Viola calearata, varying in endless shades of violet, mauve, and purple-blue, and even, at rare intervals, going to pale lilac and to pure white. Here, too, on every hand, is the exquisite Alpine Forget-me-not (Myosotis alpestris), of such heavenly blue as, surely, is never elsewhere seen than in the Alps; it is meeting in happiest communion with the paler blue of the graceful Flax (Linuia alpinum), and in happiest contrast with the golden blossoms of the Rock Rose (Helianthemum vulgare).

Now this, really, is but a rough sketch - a broad and casual impression - of the scene. Many another floral gem is here, lending its subtle beauty to the general effect. But we must be returning; time runs fleet in such a fairyland! We need not, however, retrace our steps. Let us bear to the left, along the base of these Viola-cropped slopes, and so gain yonder gully, which, if we follow it downwards, will bring us to our forest path. It will be somewhat of a scramble over the rocks and loose boulders, but we shall find plenty of fresh interest for our pains - plenty of lovely flowers with which we have not yet made acquaintance to-day.

How truly wonderful, how exquisite, it all is I To the right all purple and white, to the left all rose and gold, with blue of the heavens' own hue scattered everywhere! Although Nature 'never yields to sentiment any point of profit' - although Nature may, in herself, be devoid of every particle of sentiment - yet her effect is to produce in us abundant sentiment. After all, with humanity as with flowers, bewitching loveliness is the outcome of stern and practical necessity; and sentiment, really, there is not in the durable fabric of creation. But however that may be, here is a scene to dream amid, if ever there were one ! Here is occasion for 'that undisturbed silence of the heart which alone is perfect eloquence.' One feels with Hazlitt that these flowers are sweetest without comment; that one wants to see one's 'vague notions float like the down of the thistle before the breeze, and not to have them entangled in the briars and thorns of controversy.' Silence here, indeed, is golden. Surely here, if anywhere, the pettiness of men should evaporate, the character expand, and larger ideas take possession of the soul. 'Not to everyone,' writes Mr. John Galsworthy - 'not to everyone is it given to take a wide view of things, to look over the far, pale streams, the purple heather and moonlit pools of the wild marches, where reeds stand black against the sundown, and from long distance comes the cry of a curlew; not to everyone to gaze from steep cliffs over the wine-dark, shadowy sea, or from high mountain-side to see crowned chaos smoking with mist or gold-bright in the sun. To most it is given to watch assiduously a row of houses.' But surely here, in Nature's wildest and most orderly of lavish gardens, the 'row of houses' must vanish for the nonce while mind and soul drink of the 'largeness' of it all. Surely, too, when presently all but the memory of the scene is gone, one's 'row of houses,' erstwhile of the 'East End,' will be at least a row of pretty country villas fronted by smiling parterres.

But what a sin it seems to be walking on these flowers as we are now doing! In default, however, of a path, and in presence of such profusion, there is no other way of proceeding; we are constrained, moreover, to be 'walking, like Agag, "delicately." And here we are at the gully; and there, in the crevices of the rocks to the right, are a number of the yellow Alpine Auricula (Primula auricula), in company with a rosy band of the little Erinus alpinus. This Auricula, true representative of the Alpine flora, and prime parent of many of our garden Auriculas, is seemingly one of the few plants of which the Swiss mountain peasants take much notice, besides, of course, such herbs and flowers as they gather for medicinal purposes. Upon the roof of many a cowshed and chalet may be seen clumps of this favoured one, growing in some old soap-box or biscuit-tin - generally of English extraction.

Now, turning abruptly to the left, and descending into the gully, we find in the moist, sandy debris forming its bed quantities of the white Alpine Cress (Hutschinsia alpina), blooming among rich green clumps, scarcely yet in flower, of the golden Stonecrop Saxifrage (Saxifraga aizoides); and all along the gulley's sunny side are widespread, vivid masses of the rosy-red Rock Soapwort (Saponaria ocymoides). In profusion everywhere, but doing best on the damp and shady side, is Micheli's Daisy, the long-stalked Bellidiastrum Michelii. The blue-grey Globularia cordifolia is also here, carpeting the dried ground above; while, tucked in and about the base of the boulders over which we are scrambling, we notice, though not as yet in bloom, quantities of the yellow-green plants of the lovely Golden Marguerite (Aronicum scorpioides). Here, too, nestling plentifully with the Parsley Fern, is that fascinating little Yellow Violet (Viola biflora), looking, as always, so deliciously fresh, as if both flower and foliage had just been washed by rain.

We are now nearing the pine forest, and we had best leave the gully and 'make tracks' across the Anemone and Gentian decked slopes until we strike our path. As we clamber up the gulley's side, and just at its crest, there is a close, overhanging growth of Mountain Avens (Dryas octo-petala), a truly arresting object, clothed as it is in a purity of white and gold. Further on, as we traverse the slopes, we come upon the dense, mossy mounds of the Cushion Pink (Silene acaulis), radiant with their tiny pink blossoms. And here and there, just on the outskirts of the forest's sombre shade, is Erica carnea, the Alpine Heath, earliest of spring's mountain wonders; not now, it is true, in perfection, but lingering, as it were, to welcome us ere we descend to our hotel.

This, as has already been stated, is but an impressionist sketch, a broad and general survey of a scene which any language or any pen is, at best, inadequate to describe. The only way is to see it for oneself, and to see it again, and then again. A visit such as the one we have just paid to Nature's own garden is bound to entail a second visit, and a third and fourth; and at each successive visit the scene will be found modified in some respect. Spring is a rapid season in the Alps. Each day makes for some important change. If in a week's time we revisit the scene we have just quitted, we shall be amazed at the quick transformation of many of its details. The foliage of the plants will have developed, the grass will have grown most markedly, and the erstwhile dense carpets of rosy Primula and blue Gentian will have lost in consequence much of their vivid pristine purity. The flowers of the Anemone will be turning rusty brown, and will be falling, giving place (in the case of alpina) to the beautiful feathery seed-heads, and the Crocus and Soldanella will have altogether disappeared. But this does not mean that the ravishing and prolific reign of colour will be on the verge of ending; it merely means that other beauties, equally profuse, equally colourfull, will be replacing those that are passing. Orchids will be springing up everywhere in varieties according to the ground and situation. On the more level, marshy stretch, where was the Primula farinosa, will be Orchis sambucina, the Elder-smelling Orchis, varying from pale yellow to deep blood-red; on the slopes, where was Anemone alpina, will be the sweet-scented Gymnadenia odoratissima and G. conopea, together with the red and lilac Orchis globosa; while almost everywhere will be appearing the curiously dark, claret-coloured heads of the Vanilla Orchid (Nigritella angustifolia). On the slopes, too, there will be hosts of the graceful paper-white sprays of St. Bruno's or Paradise Lily (Paradisia Liliastrum); while the rocks will be creamy-white with a wealth of Saxifraga Aizoon, one of the loveliest of Saxifrages. No; spring has no lack of successive substitutes. It is only when Crepis aurea, the sienna-red Dandelion or Golden Hawksbeard, begins to appear, and summer is hurriedly commencing, that spring's ubiquity and profusion of purest, freshest colour begins to wane.

As has been said, there are many resorts in the Alps where these delights of spring are at the very door - instance the Col de la Forclaz, above Martigny, in the Rhone Valley. Here, although it is about 4,500 feet up, or about 1,500 feet higher than Champery and Chateau-d'Cex, one can, if the season be normal, comfortably sojourn towards the beginning or middle of May, and for those who wish to be living on the very threshold of Alpine spring life few places can be more desirable. From the very windows of the hotel (the proprietor of which, by the way, once had the honour of carrying Queen Alexandra, then Princess of Wales, across freshly-fallen snow on the Col de Balme) one can look out upon slopes teeming with the large sulphur-yellow Anemone (Anemone sulfurea), here growing in such manner as to give strength to the doubts expressed in some quarters as to whether this Anemone is really a separate species, or only a granitic form of A. Alpina; for on these slopes are some white-flowered forms as well as many which are but slightly suffused with yellow, and the backs of the sepals have some of the blue tinge which is characteristic of alpina. On these slopes, too, if one strolls out, as one may, after breakfast, will be found quantities of Gentiana Kochiana and verna; also the blue, white, and pink Hepatica, on the fringe of the forest which crowns the slopes; also the Box-leaved Milkwort (Polygala Chamoebuxus) and its little blue relative, P. alpestris; also the deep, rich blue Veronica saocatilis, the graceful Thesiurn alpinurti, the golden Genista sagittalis and Hippocrepis comosa, the curious Moonwort (Botrychium lunaria), the Mountain Cudweed (Antennaria dioica), and many another gem growing amongst bushes of the Alpine Rose - not the Alpenrose or Rhododendron, but the true Rosa alpina, the rose without a thorn. And these slopes, as soon as the Anemone is passing, will be crowded with Orchids in six or seven varieties, all in flower with the Rose.

Primula Farinosa, The Oxlip And Marsh Marigold, With The Argentine In The Background. Les Plans. April.

On the other side of the hotel, covering a picturesque pasture belonging partly to Martigny, there is a profuse and varied flora, in many respects differing from that just described. Here one will find Soldanella alpina and Gentiana verna, together with Micheli's Daisy, the Bell-Gentian, that curious Alpine Coltsfoot, Homogyne alpina, and the little brown-and-green Frog Orchid, growing in great quantity among the Bilberries and Strawberries, and presently to be replaced by St. Bruno's Lily, Arnica, and a perfect sea of other flowers. And the lawn-like turf of the pasture proper is a veritable joy, with the purple Viola, the Antennaria, the little Star-Gentian {Gentiana nivalis), the Rock Rose, the small canary-yellow Dandelion, the Bell-Gentian, the Vernal Gentian (of which there are white, lilac, and Cambridge-blue forms), and the striking pagodalike pyramids of the Alpine Bugle (Ajuga pyra-midalis), coloured so aesthetically with brown-madder and blue. Of pure luxury one could desire nothing more; for one may stroll out and feast whenever the spirit dictates - in the heat of the day, when the call of the Cuckoo is echoing through the pine forests and the Robin-like note of the Redstart comes cheerfully from some rustic fence or heap of stones, or in the cool of the evening, when the Blackbird is singing amid the golden showers of the wild Laburnum, the Ghost Moth is performing its strange, giddy dance over the Anemones, Geraniums, and Grasses, and the lovely Glacier des Grands is rosy tinted with the 'afterglow. One can pass the sunny days in luxurious dreaming' on one's back in a bed of Rhododendrons' - for the Rhododendron is here - dreaming until the dinner-bell breaks in upon one's reveries, and calls one to a repast more mortal and substantial.

But dreaming of what? Dreaming of the flowers, and of beyond the flowers? For the effect of their beauty is to translate one far above their beauty. Material as they are, unsentimental as is their existence, they render one doubly immaterial and doubly sentimental.

But dreaming of what? Dreaming of the time when the cattle will be here, eating off this crop of Alpine loveliness? Perhaps. For, with June, the day will soon arrive when the cattle-bells will chime in all their fascinating discord over these selfsame pastures, and then good-bye to the flowers hereabouts, except in out-of-reach nooks and corners. What the cows do not eat off the goats will nibble down, and where the animals are not allowed to wander the peasant comes with his scythe and makes his hay. Then, for the flowers, one must go away, up higher - up on the last steep, grassy slopes, and up around the glaciers. There, to be sure, will one find fresh wonders, but nothing to compare in abundance of pure colour with the wonders of the spring.

And - oh, the pity of it! - at this late season it is, when the cattle and the scythe have gained disastrous footing, that the majority of visitors arrive. And when, after their holiday, they return home, they do so thinking they have tasted of the chiefest glories of the Alps. Oh, Ignorance! sometimes, maybe, thy name spells bliss, but only, mark ye, sometimes!

CHAPTER III. THE CROCUS, AND SOME DREAMING

The dreamer's season par excellence is the spring. It is then that his dreams arise as irresistibly as the flowers - and, in large measure, because of the flowers. From time immemorial spring, and the flowers of spring, have given the poet more occasion to sing than perhaps has any other time or event of the year. Nor do his dreamy songs seem out of placed Quite the contrary: one accepts them as of the very essentials of the season. And this is the more remarkable when one thinks of what spring really means: the breaking into energy of business, stern and uncompromising, of every living thing. It is the season whose rousing call is to the strenuous worker, and amongst these, obviously, to the dreamy poet. He hears the call, understands it, and, after his own fashion, answers it. He, then, is one of the necessary workers summoned - proof that what is called dreaming, however low it may rank in the estimation of many, has often a place of high and useful purpose in the economy of the world's progress - a place often higher than that of potato-planting (never forgetting, however, that all usefulness is relative, and therefore incomparable).

Now, among all the dreamer's happy hunting-grounds, none can rank higher than the Alps - and, too, the Alps in spring. There is an appeal in this direction as irresistible as it is wide. Upon all hands, and in all things, is striking food for 'Thoughts that do often lie too deep for tears, too deep for laughter, too deep for anything more demonstrative than dreaming. Wander forth in the latter days of March or the early days of April up the mountain-side. The sun is brilliant in a cloudless sky, and the Alps, decked in the snows of December, stand superbly mysterious, bathed in a blue fine-weather haze. Spring is afoot, and standing upon the threshold of the Future. Winter's strictest rigours are relaxing. The southward-facing rocks are baring themselves under the sun's increasing and inspiring presence. Numberless patches of yellow-brown turf dapple the lower slopes and pastures, giving the foreground of the landscape a piebald aspect. It is Winter's mantle fast becoming threadbare; and there, through the worn-out parts, hundreds upon hundreds of frail crocuses are peeping, dainty in their new-born white and purple.

'Though not a whisper of her voice he hear, The buried bulb does know The signals of the year, And hails far Summer with his lifted spear.'

It is a moving sight, these frail and lonely legions standing amid such threatening wastes of snow. How radiant and gleaming they are under the sun's encouragement! How brave of them to venture thus early from their hiding! And yet do they carry themselves with no air of bravado. Their dainty bearing is the personification of sweet humility. Their meekness, however, has no taint of trembling. Confidence, begot of duty faithfully performed, lends them a calm and serenity which is positively infectious. Unconscious of all worth, they are a thousand times the worthier and fairer. Indifference, though, is foreign to their nature; and Self has so nice a place as to give full aid to the best of purpose. Meekly dauntless, unselfishly self-assertive, truly do they come to quicken the hopes and gladden the hearts of winter - logged mortals, setting these latter a lesson well worth bearing in mind.

The impulse is to revisit again and again this scene of promise, and watch with intent its gradual realization. But here, in these regions at this season, few things are so certain as the uncertain. Winter has still a living voice in these affairs. Smarting under a sense of its waning rule, vindictively it summons up the remnants of its breath, and hurls a blighting blizzard athwart the scene of promise, nipping the vernal Crocus with its icy blast, and crushing it beneath a foot of snow.

Intrepid flower! You recked naught of 'The Shepheard's Calendar,' and thus 'When the shining sunne laugheth once, You deemen the spring is come attonce.'

But the sun is not yet master of the situation; again 'Comes the breme winter with chamfred browes, Full of wrinckles and frostic furrowes, Drerily shooting his stormy-darte, Which cruddles the blood and pricks the harte.'

Unhappy flower! So much for your pains; so much for duty done! Coming thus intrepidly to brighten a drear world, you have been rudely and contemptuously treated as a thing of inept conceit, of inflated importance, fit only to be disfigured and crushed for your presumption. Herald of prospective floral wonders and rich harvests for Man and his flocks, intent upon an errand of good cheer, you emerged meekly fearless from a safe and snug seclusion, only to be met by Winter in its 'crabbed old age.' in its unseemly death-throes.

Gentian A Verna And The Glacier De Plan-Neve, Les Plans. April.

Ah well! that is the poetry and the pathos of the matter; what is the bald, important truth ? Just this - as the Crocus itself would tell us: our pathos is in large part bathos; and the fate so often overtaking this charming denizen of the Alps is typical of the universal order of things, so severe, so maligned, and yet so inevitably right - an order of seeming injustice which is all the time making for justice. Creation is the child of severity and strictness, not of sentiment. And the child is as capable as it is by reason of this stern upbringing. Nature's injustice is sentiment, and does not exist. But because there is no sentiment, this is not proof of Nature's unkindness. Nature is kind because she is stern. Happiness lies in efficiency. In creating efficient capacity in things Nature shows her kindness: for she creates happiness.

Contemplating this demure and dainty little flower, and meditating upon its condition, one can scarcely escape assimilating something of the happiness and serenity of purpose which pervades it and so much helps it to thrive in the face of such difficulties. Apparently overwhelmed, and its very-existence blighted and crippled, this is not really the case. Patient perseverance has made it a match for the weather; adversity has given it amazing power. Winter may do its worst, and yet this apparently frail little plant not only survives all attacks, but prospers.

'When lowly, with a broken neck, The Crocus lays her cheek to mire,' she does so with easy resignation and content. It is possible there is even a smile - a smile with a world of deep meaning in it - playing about her little face: for she knows that she has conquered; she knows that she has overcome Winter, though this latter may think otherwise, and exult accordingly.

No sooner does the snow retire again than the Crocus, although hampered with the rotting wreckage of its despised blossom, at once throws up its grass-like leaves and commences assiduously to draw in stores to replenish its depleted strength, and to lay up in its earth-protected body provision of energy for future contests with assaulting circumstance. Prematurely cut down in the midst of its loveliest effort, it perseveringly bides its time, gathering in those forces, meanwhile, which shall enable it to make a further brave attempt the next year.

But this is not all: its contented smile means more than this. Through ages of ceaseless striving with circumstance, it has evolved so nice a capacity in itself as to be able to successfully defy circumstance in very large and important measure. For, by infinite patience and dogged tenacity of purpose, it has arrived at keeping its seed-producing chamber beneath the soil at this inclement season. It has caused the stem of its flower to be a connecting-duct between its seed-vessels and its pollen-bearing stamen, so that, brief as may be its bloom's perfection, the early, eager bee, fly, or beetle may successfully achieve the beneficent work of inoculation; or, even should no insects be about, the stigmas, of their own contriving, dust themselves with pollen from the anthers. Should, then, its flower and stem be soon after beaten to the ground, the process of seed - development goes forward below, and will be brought to fruition above the ground under later and more favourable auspices. Thus, through faithful and consistent endeavour to conquer its disabilities, it has evolved, and maintains, an astonishing power for the due expression of its necessity in the face of heavy odds. Surely its smile of equanimity at Winter's threats of extermination is amply justified!

What more inspiring than this cheerful optimism - optimism begot of a sure capacity? Small need, here, for pity and pathos! Better engaged are we in following this little flower's lead by looking facts in the face with that true pessimism, three parts optimism, which nourishes a due and proper energy. For thus may we acquire, as has acquired the Crocus, such efficiency as alone means soundest happiness.

Noting the unconcerned and enviable content of this efficient plant under conditions which, with all our boasted intelligence and resource, would appal us, must we not, in all conscience, exclaim, as Wordsworth exclaimed:

'And I must think, do all I can, That there was pleasure there.'

' If this belief from heaven be sent, If such be Nature's holy plan, Have I not reason to lament What man has made of man?'

CHAPTER IV. WHERE DO 'ALPINES' BEGIN?

Where should the line for Alpine plants be drawn? The question is not always an easy one to answer. So much depends upon the nature and situation of the ground, as well as upon the nature and history of the plant of which one may be speaking. In the first instance, a common line of altitude it is impossible to draw across the Alps. In some situations Alpine vegetation will descend much lower than in others. As M. Flahault, the eminent French botanist, says: 'Dans une meme chaine, les plantes de la montagne apparaissent a des niveaux tres variables, suivant les versants.' There is a very striking instance of this in the mountains at the entrance to the Rhone Valley. On one hand is Champery, by the side of the Dent du Midi; on the other is Villars-sur-Ollon, by the side of the Dent de Morcles. Champe'ry is at an altitude of about 3,500 feet, and Villars at about 4,250 feet, and yet the vegetation immediately around the former is far more Alpine in character than that immediately around the latter. At Champe'ry one can find Alpines such as Gentiana Kochiana and Lathyrus luteus within fifteen or twenty minutes of the hotels; whereas at Villars, which is situated some 650 feet higher than Champery, one must walk quite an hour and a half farther up before one finds oneself in touch with such Alpine conditions.

And if it is impossible to draw a common line of altitude for Alpine plants, it is equally impossible to draw a strict and just line of distinction among these plants; all that can be drawn is but a relatively just line. Many usurpers are sharing the Alpine throne, and sharing it, too, with superb and easy effrontery. There is, of course, a distinctive flora with which one has no hesitation in dealing, but this flora lives frequently cheek by jowl with immigrants - immigrants making themselves perfectly at home, and adopting most successfully the ways of all that is indigenous - and these immigrants it is by no means always easy to separate from their companions.

Some plants seem to be very shy of travel, whilst others prove themselves to be, as it were, veritable 'globe-trotters.' Some, such as the common Primrose and the Squill (Scilla bifolia), positively refuse to wander far upwards from their home, whilst others, like the common Coltsfoot and the Stinging-Nettle, are astonishingly daring travellers in Alpine altitudes. The prevailing tendency appears to be upwards rather than downwards, as if the flowers were moved by human aspirations, and sought for an ever purer clime. Whereas quite a large number of lowland plants climb with seeming ease and impunity, true Alpines do not show corresponding ease in descending. The grosser conditions of the civilized zone appear to unnerve and undo them, and they languish and die in the lap of unwonted luxury. Luxury kills more surely than hardship, and these sturdy children of harsh conditions succumb to an easier state of things. It may be that their greatest difficulty is to cope efficiently with the excess of dampness. They have been evolved in harmony with conditions which are dry for a good three-quarters of the year. They are the product of what for lowland plants would be drought, for only when the snows are melting, or when there are storms and mists, do they obtain moisture. Drainage is rapid, and almost immediately the ground is again dry. This it is that makes the growing of Alpines (even the Alpine marsh plants) in England often no easy matter; unless they can be protected from what to them is Winter's superfluity of dampness, the result must lean largely towards failure. And this it is, no doubt, that militates greatly against them leaving their Alpine home of their own accord. But vice versa the difficulty does not appear to be so pronounced, and lowland plants have, seemingly, a far greater facility for adapting themselves to altered conditions. If Alpine circumstance may be taken as one of comparative refinement, then it would appear that it is more feasible, healthy, and proper to climb up to that sphere and to adopt its conditions than it is to quit it and descend to a lower plane; which makes very good philosophy for man as well as for plants.

But this state of things causes it to be often no easy matter to frame any hard and fast rule for the distinguishing of Alpines as a class. How be strict and dogmatic in this regard with, for instance, the Mealy Primula, the Sticky Primula, the Daffodil, the Hepatica, the Dog's-tooth Violet, or the Vernal Crocus? They are flowers of the Swiss plain and Alp alike. The Mealy Primula is as profuse about

Villeneuve and Vouvry, at the entrance to the Rhone Valley, as it is on the Col des Mosses (about 4,500 feet) or the high plateaux immediately beneath the cliffs of the Gumfluh; the Sticky Primula brightens the rocks about Vernayaz as it brightens those about the Col de la Gueulaz (some 6,000 feet); the Daffodil is apparently as much at home at Champéry or at Saas-Fee as it is in the neighbourhood of Morges on the Lake of Geneva; the Hepatica is as flourishing in the forests around Lac Champex (about 4,600 feet) as it is in the woods around Aigle or Bex; the Dog's-tooth Violet is as happy near the Glacier de Trient (some 5,000 feet) as it is in the Bois de Chillon, near Territet; while the Vernal Crocus is no less abundant in the vicinity of the Grand St. Bernard or on the Col de Coux (some 5,700 feet) than it is in the fields at the back of Lausanne.

Primula V1scosa Above Vernayaz, In The Rhone Valley, With The Grand Combin In The Distance. End Of April.

All this makes often for difficulty in drawing the necessary line, and in deciding what plants to leave inside that line and what to leave without. One notices the presence of this difficulty in the numerous books on the flora of the Alps. Why, for example, should Trollius europceus find a place in these books and none be given to the Stinging-Nettle? Both are to be found around the glacier and down in the plains. Is it that the bright golden Globe Flower carries itself with all the air of an Alpine, and so is allowed to pass in amongst the élite, and is it that the Nettle's more vulgar, plebeian appearance is a too heavy handicap in this regard? Certainly our old friend the Nettle - no matter what Jean Jacques Rousseau may have found in its favour as a garden plant - lacks Alpine refinement, and looks sadly out of place amid Alpine scenery, although that faithful companion, the Small Tortoiseshell Butterfly, may do its charming, extra-vivid best to make amends for the graceless intrusion of its ill-conditioned food-plant.

There is a curious fact about the Alpine wanderings of the Nettle which is worthy of notice. Although it is ready to sting him upon the slightest provocation, this Nettle appears really amicably disposed towards man. It seems to love to be with him, and to go where he goes, even following him up to the glaciers. For, as far as I have observed, it is not found in a really wild and lonely state in Alpine altitudes, but only where the soil has been disturbed by the peasant and his beasts, Around cattle-sheds and chalets, however remote these may be, one can generally count upon finding this Nettle; but away from all human habitation or human influence one never meets with it; at least, that is my experience. And how does it get to these regions? What subterfuge does it employ in order to accompany man upon such long journeys? Can it be the winds or the birds which aid it? It may be that its seeds travel with the peasant and his cattle - on the boots, the clothing, and the belongings of the former, or on the hoofs and in the hairy coats of the latter. This method of transport is by no means uncommon; many a plant now found in Britain is believed to have come over with the Romans in some such fashion. Any way, there it usually is, close beside the peasant's dwelling, 6,000 to 7,000 feet, maybe, above its ancient home. Perhaps, then, this is one good reason why it has no recognized place among the Alpine 'upper ten.' But why should not such reasons as these debar the Globe Flower from inclusion among the elect? May not this plant also (and, for that matter, many another plant) have travelled upwards in some such fashion as the Nettle?

Who shall tell? With winds and air-currents as violent and erratic as in Switzerland, anything in the nature of seed distribution is possible. But however that may be, it does not appear to be a point which counts. The point which appears to count, at any rate in the present instance, is that the Globe Flower shows a certain independence. It is to be found, up to some 7,000 feet, on damp pastures, sunny or shady, wellnigh anywhere in the Alps, whereas the Nettle does not roam on its own account; it does not spread to every desirable nook and corner of the Alps - indeed, as circumstanced in the Alps, it can scarcely be called wild; it seems, really, to detest Alpine conditions, and to hug whatever it can find of the grossness of lowland, civilized soil. Perhaps, then, this want of independence bars the Nettle, if not from admittance, then from official recognition within the charmed circle of Alpine vegetation.

But independence is not always the necessary passport, or what are we to say of the Dock? Here is a subject which offers us another instance of the apparent attachment of some plants to man, especially when they find themselves in Alpine places. Unlike the Nettle, however, the Dock is admitted to books on the Alpine flora, and is there given as Rumex alpinus. But what is the plant's origin? What is its history? Does its present habit of sociability with man date, like that of the swallow, from prehistoric times, from the times of the cave-dweller? There are certain grounds for doubting the strict legality of its title, just as there are grounds for doubting the title of Myosotis alpestris, though in the case of the Dock these doubts are perhaps graver. There is some evidence of the Dock having been planted expressly in times past - indeed, I have met with a kind of tradition to this effect among the peasantry. It is a useful plant to the montagnard (although its dry flower-stem is abomination in his hay). He employs it as a medicine for himself; and not only is it excellent fodder, in the green state, for the pigs (and the cowherd or peasant frequently brings a pig or two with him into the mountains for summer), but its leaves are still often used to wrap around butter to keep it fresh, and in times past, before the introduction of special linen for this purpose, the custom was general - upon much the same principle as, in the Ardennes, the Nettle is used for keeping fish fresh.

Then, again, why should Tussilago Farfara, the common Coltsfoot, be excluded from books on Alpine flowers? The Coltsfoot suffers from no such disabilities as the Nettle. It is a lonely, independent wanderer, making itself as much at home in the moraine of a glacier as it does upon any rough ground down in the plains. Is its exclusion a case of familiarity breeding contempt; and is this, too, the real reason for snubbing the Nettle?

There are, in fact, no lack of examples which might be quoted in support of this indictment. Even Gentiana verna is not altogether free from suspicion, it being frequently met with in the lower valleys, or, as they are termed in Switzerland, the plains, though, with all due apologies to Byron, it cannot be accused of having been seen by the Prisoner of Chillon from his cell! I have found it, and its beautiful white form also, by the Rhone, at Lavey-les-Bains, near St. Maurice (about 1,300 feet altitude); and Mr. H. Stuart Thompson, in one of his luminous articles contributed to the Teacher's Times, mentions this Gentian as having been found by him 'as low as 1,600 feet, near the beautiful lake of Annecy in Savoie.'Gentiana lutea, too, I have found blooming freely by a stone-quarry quite close to Villeneuve. But I suppose we must take it as quite out of the question to attempt to impeach these two plants, and to bar them from inclusion with true Alpines. Their place on the list of the elect is secure; we cannot spare them - as we can the Nettle!

Enough has been said, however, to show that there is some very real difficulty in drawing any hard and fast line among Alpine plants without doing some injustice to either one side or the other of the line. The fact is, no such lines can, in strictness, be drawn anywhere in Nature; such lines can only stand for purely utilitarian purposes. In 'The Face of Nature,' Dr. C. T. Ovenden declares, in his chapter on 'Vegetable Life,' that 'it is easy to say that man stands at the head of creation, that the animals are lower, and the vegetables lower still, but our difficulty commences when we try to draw a sharp line of distinction between the low forms of animal life and those which are vegetable.' But are we not becoming aware that our difficulty begins before this? Are we not beginning to feel that it is easy enough to say, but not at all easy to prove, that our difficulty about drawing a sharp line of demarcation arises only when dealing with the lower forms of life? We feel to-day that there is a 'missing link' between man and the apes, and we are continually coming upon links which connect those creations which stand on one side of some old, dogmatic line with those which stand on the other side. Gradually, but surely, are we erasing these lines for all ultimate purposes; gradually, but surely, are we coming to recognize them for what assuredly they are - useful, even necessary, but ultimately unscientific and untruthful. Although Dr. Ovenden finds a difficulty in sharply dividing vegetable life from the lower forms of animal life, yet further on he has no difficulty in speaking of organic and inorganic life; and this, I think, is an apt illustration of our growing recognition of what will, some day, be a general difficulty. The difficulty with regard to animal and vegetable life did not exist for us a little while back, and presently we shall recognize difficulties in the way of scientifically dividing organic from inorganic life.

Let me quote another author on this point - Mr. Edward Step. In the introductory chapter to his 'The Romance of Wild Flowers,' he says: 'It may be fairly claimed that during the last half-century our prevailing notions respecting plant life have been greatly modified, and, concerning flowering plants, have been entirely changed. Fifty years ago there could be found very few botanists who were not satisfied with the generalizations crystallized in the Linnsean axiom: '"Stones grow, Vegetables grow and live, Animals grow, live, and feel."

There, in less than a dozen words, was a handy and easily-remembered formula, serving as a kind of touchstone which, when applied to any doubtful organism, would detect whether it were plant or animal. But other times, other methods: the Linnaean formula is absolutely obsolete to-day.'

And so must this broadening of our views continue as our powers of perception and appreciation become greater. It is our ignorance which enables us to draw dogmatic lines with so much complacency. We are on little more than bowing terms with evolution; our practical conception of it is as yet more casual than intimate. With evolution accepted in its logical fulness as a thorough article of faith, how, in strictness, draw the line anywhere in circumstance which must be one unbroken chain? Science will some day oblige us to know that such distinctions as 'something' and 'nothing,' organic' and 'inorganic,' are simply useful terms relative to the exigencies of finite thought and speech. We can, and we shall, always think more than we say, but every day we say more and more what we think. And in time we shall not only think, but convincedly and intelligently speak, of creation as an indivisible whole - divisible only temporarily, and for our own mortal convenience.

Alpine Garden (La Thomasia) At Pont De Nant, Above Les Plans, With The Glacier De Martinet. Middle Of May.

In dealing, then, with Alpine flowers, it is necessary to draw some line of demarcation; but, at the same time, and with regard to a number of plants, we may know that the line is only rough and relative - relative to that need for cutting up Creation into sections which is so inevitable an element in our means for obtaining even approximate understanding of the whole.

CHAPTER V. CERTAIN CHARACTERISTICS OF ALPINE PLANTS

That which is bound to strike the observer at once about Alpine plants is the large size and profusion of their flowers in comparison with the dimensions of the plants themselves. All about them, except their blossoms, appears on such a restrained scale. Generally they are of a dwarf and stunted nature - a small moss-like tuft or compact, leafy rosette, hugging the soil - whilst their blossoms are either so numerous as to completely hide them under a wealth of colour - as in the case of the Moss Campion (Silene rupestris) and the Bastard Cress (Thlaspi rotundifolium) - or are so large as to equal and often surpass the size of the plant itself - as in the case of the Bell-Gentian (Gentiana Kochiana) and the Alpine Viola (Viola calcarata). It is as if their whole energy was given up to making themselves as attractive and irresistible as possible to the bees and butterflies. And this, no doubt, is their aim - or shall we say, in view of Mr. E. K. Robinson's theory, this, no doubt, is a large part of their present aim? Insects are not so numerous here as down in the plains. Moths and butterflies there certainly are in quantities, but bees and flies (for all that tourists may say about cattle-flies!) are far more scarce. Time, too, is shorter. The blossoming season is more contracted. 'Hay' must be made while the sun shines; every effort put forth to salute to good purpose 'the passing moment as it flies.' Hence one very good reason, one would think, for the lavish, gorgeous colour which so dominates the verdure, and is so distinctive a feature of the Alpine landscape.

I say 'one would think,' because Mr. E. K. Robinson, in The Countryside, has formulated a theory which, if essentially correct, will oblige us to modify considerably what Darwin, Lord Avebury, and others have taught us to believe. Mr. Robinson holds that 'the real, primary, and original meaning of the colours, markings, nectar, and scents of flowers is not to attract insects, but to deter grazing and browsing animals.' And I see no reason to fall out with this entirely, or, indeed, in any large measure. Efficient capacity for self-protection is the key-note of Creation's prosperity.

Creation is thoroughly on the defensive, or it would not thrive, and anything - any attribute or contrivance - of docile purpose is, so to speak, thoroughly policed and fenced about with barbed wire. Hence flowers can scarcely be wholly and meekly inviting. Yet we are children of extremes, and it were well to bear in mind how much we are liable to rush from black to white, from yes to no, and how adverse we are to compromise. Possibly we should do best, and we should credit the flowers with greater efficiency, if we accepted both the old and the new theory - that is to say, if we contrived a strong amalgam of the truths which, to my mind, undoubtedly exist in both. It seems possible that the colour, form, and scent of flowers may repel in some directions and invite in others - may, in fact, have a dual purpose, and may have had such purpose from the first. What proof is there for Mr. Robinson's suggestion that bees, butterflies, and other insects only 'appeared upon the scene' after the flowers had developed their form, colour, odour, and nectar as protection from browsing animals? - a suggestion which implies that browsing animals are of longer standing than insects.

Although everything in this world has its enemies, nothing in this world has only enemies.

Everything, then, may be utterly capable of defence, and yet have a smile for suitable occasions. An element of reciprocity is, and must always have been, the mainstay of every condition and circumstance, and it is essential that flowers should be, and should always have been, able to smile as well as to scowl. It would never have done for them to be all bristles, and without a warm corner in their hearts for whatever was deserving of it. They would have suffered, probably to extinction, had this been so, as everything of a solely bristling nature must inevitably suffer. Even the ferocious alligator has a kindly tolerance and welcome for a certain little bird, for whom the saurian's fearsome armament has no terrors.

For this reason I incline to think that the old adage, 'What is one man's meat is another man's poison,' applies equally to flowers. Following the rule for efficiency and prosperity, a plant can only benefit through being poisonous for one visitor and wholesome for another; or, putting it in another way, tastes differ, and therefore a plant will, with one and the same gesture, both repulse and beckon. We have all heard of the man who could not live in the country because of 'the wretched smell of violets.' It is a case in point. This man, evidently, was no friend of the violets: he would have trampled upon them, destroyed them - he was repelled by them; yet there is many a man who is friendly, who will tend and cultivate them and rejoice in their scent - whom, in fact, the violets invite. In short, I incline to the belief that, by one and the same manifestation, a flower is both repulsive and seductive, and that it has been so from the beginning, and in the very best interests of the plant. Mr. Robinson says, 'Nothing is ever wasted in Nature'; and I think we may add that nothing in Nature is ever simple. That is to say, there is nothing in Nature which is not double-edged: nothing whose properties or capacities are not many-sided in effect and purpose. Why should flowers be, or have been, an exception to this complex efficiency of design?

Moreover, it seems just possible that Alpines may have something to say in modification of Mr. Robinson's theory. According to a logical application of that theory, the more brilliantly coloured, more profusely produced, and, in many cases, more highly scented and heavily honeyed blossoms of Alpines should go to prove that there exists in the Alps a browsing fauna which is more numerous than in the plains. Whereas, actually, it is the other way about, and there are remarkably fewer browsing animals in the Alps, both in variety and in number. No, we are not forgetting the goat, which is so numerous, and which, certainly, is not affrighted by the awful aspect of the Alpine flora! But 'we must discount the goat and other domesticated animals as guides to natural conditions,' says Mr. Robinson; and I think we may agree. Civilization breeds 'acquired' tastes, 'depraved' tastes, 'unnatural' tastes - tastes which can be little criterion for the conditions under which the flowers developed the essential characters of their blossoms. Dismissing, then, the domesticated cow, goat, and sheep, the danger from browsing animals becomes very small indeed; and I doubt if, since Alpines have been such as they are, the danger has ever been much greater. This leaves us face to face with the possibility that these lovely plants suffer from what hitherto has been looked upon as a modern and human malady - 'nerves'! But perhaps the characteristics of their blossoms are legacies from the dim past age when the mammoth roamed the snows and ice of the world; and now, in these less exciting days, the colour, scent, form, and nectar of these flowers have been amiably retained for the delight and use of the insects! It is as though swords had been turned into ploughshares!

Gentiana Kochiana, G. Verna, And Silene Acaulis At The Col De La Forclaz, Above Martigny, In The Rhone Valley. Early In June.

But, fascinating as this subject is, and deserving as it is of deep and lengthy study, we must pass on to another characteristic, obviously less noticeable, though none the less remarkable - the roots of these Alpine wonders. In their battle against the fierce winds and excessive dryness, these plants send roots down to astonishing depths - astonishing when compared with what is to be seen of the plants above ground. A little tuft or rosette of leaves, the size round of a five-shilling piece, will often have a system of roots extending a foot or more down into the soil or into the depths of some crevice in the rock, with ramifications in all possible directions. Nor can this surprise us when we come to study the conditions under which they live the year round. These roots, gathering in the moisture when and where they may, are the plants' larders and store-rooms. Think of how many months they spend in obliteration from the world. Buried often for some nine months in the year beneath the snow, they needs must have well-stocked larders to draw upon. Often, even, it may be some few years before they see the sun and breathe the mountain air again. This, to some, will sound a Munchausen-like exaggeration, but it is only the simple truth. It is not every summer that the sun has power to rid the sheltered little Alpine valleys of the winter snow; often must many a plant beget its soul in patience for at least two years, comforting itself, 'in the mad maze of hope,' with thoughts of all it will accomplish during the brief interval of sun and air when it will once more put forth its flowers.

I remember, on one notable occasion, coming upon a more than ordinary instance of this reawakening of Alpine plant-life from an abnormally long seclusion. It was in August, and late in August, in the little, secluded valley (the French have a better word - vallon) of Susanfe, at the back of the Dent du Midi, and between that mountain and the Glacier de Soix. There, in an extensive hollow, lying beneath the rocks and cliffs which mount to the glacier above, was a large bed of ice and snow doing its best to melt and disappear whilst yet there was a chance. This ice was evidently not of one winter's making. Probably there is always more or less of it here - according to the sway which summer can obtain. And yet here, all around the edge of this ice, in the rusty, sodden turf, were springing up, with all the haste of pent-up eagerness, quantities of the year's earliest flowers. Even away under the hollow dome of icy snow, which resembled the snout of some miniature glacier, tiny plants could be discerned already busily developing their bloom-buds. Here, late in August, was very early spring! Here was the Crocus and the Vernal Gentian, the Solda-nella, Viola, and Oxlip. Here, too, was Trollius europceus, the Globe Flower, and Ranunculus alpestris - not, as lower down in the normal spring-time, making their usual growth of stem and leaf before opening their flowers, but hurrying up at once their blossoms on the shortest of thick, fleshy stalks. Here was no time for easy loitering; here was but to do - or die! In another month, perhaps less, snow might be expected to be again in possession of the scene; and then for another nine weary months of seclusion - perhaps, even, for another two live-long years! Truly, it is a state of things which, much on all-fours with that of the traditional toad and beetle, cannot but give pause for thought and wonder, and the more so when we think that there, under that remaining mass of ice, are yet more hundreds of little Alpine plants which can never hope to see the light of day this year!

This is an extreme, but by no means rare, instance of those conditions which compel Alpines to be as they are - for the most part all root and flower. Small occasion have they for the elaboration of much foliage. Nor is it to their advantage to attempt much show in that direction. This is the region, if there be any such particular region in wild Nature, of concentrated efficiency: a region where all energy is entirely practical: a region where the scarcity of humidity and the frequent occurrence of tempests, the presence of a most 'personal' sun during the day and of very keen frost during the night, renders the striving after great stature and much foliage a positive madness. But if anywhere in this world unadulterated sanity reigns, it is here; here, if nowhere else, the one absorbing interest is in keeping an ever open and alert eye on the main chance, and in employing such chance without hesitation.

And happiness is the outcome - as complete and real a happiness as is to be found in this world of unsatisfied satisfaction. Give these plants more 'comforts' - such conditions as we look upon as 'home comforts' - and we at once upset their happiness. 'Home comforts' they have in abundance. A winter of nine months spent under snow, a summer of feverish haste, of alternate frost and burning sunshine, of storm and drought - these are their 'home comforts,' satisfying and indispensable, as real a set of comforts as any we ourselves possess down in the plains. Do we think to know better, and to urge upon these happy Alpines some of our ideas of happiness and comfort, we only end in making them miserable, and in showing once again our traditional and egregious conceit.

Almost anywhere in the Alps at an altitude of between 3,000 and 5,000 feet we may meet with striking illustrations of the Alpines' dislike and dread of civilized 'comforts.' Almost anywhere at this altitude we may find pastures dressed annually with manure by the peasants, running side by side with others that are untouched in this regard and are used the season round as grazing-ground for the cows. Perhaps a rough wall of stones, or one of the rustic Alpine fences, will separate the two pastures; but such boundaries are not necessary, except to keep the cattle from the pasture dressed for producing hay, for the line of demarcation is most distinctly marked by the vegetation. The dressed enclosure is positively rank in its growth compared with the close-cropped appearance of the neighbouring ground. Not that there is anything remarkable in this fact of itself. The remarkable thing is that on the dressed field and slopes there is an almost total absence of all the truer Alpines, It is useless looking here for any of the blue Gentians, for instance, or for the Viola, the Soldanella, the Antennaria, or the Alpine Avens. They have long since fled in dismay at man's unnecessary attentions. Although the Crocus does not seem to particularly mind one way or the other (and it can scarcely be considered a pure-blooded Alpine), it is as much as a few sulphur or white Anemones can do to withstand the 'comfort' heaped upon them by civilization. And yet, just over on the other side of the boundary, there will be a wealth of Gentian, Viola, and Anemone, and of a score or more of other Alpines, disporting themselves in the greatest happiness, and showing their disdain and repugnance for human ideas of careful luxe and kind consideration.

It is an object-lesson, and one that should be borne in mind by those who attempt the culture of Alpines in England. Born in hardship, as children of hardship, Alpine plants have so attuned themselves to harsh conditions as to make of these the very mainspring of their joy in life. Only there, amid such conditions, are they at their fullest ease; only there can they smile as we know them capable of smiling. Those wild, stern places of so angry, hard, forbidding circumstance are most obviously their most precious birthright. Be it in winter, be it in summer, be it in storm, or be it in sunshine, these Alpine wilds are their well-loved home - aye, and more than home, their Paradise.

CHAPTER VI. SUMMER IN THE ALPS

The irresponsible harmony of a hundred cow-bells; a like but thinner music from a hundred head of goats; the sharp, strident clacking of the coachmen's whips as diligence and carriage wend their way up from the plain; the weird notes from the great goat-horn as the goatherd gathers his scattered flock together from the rocky heights above; the constant lowing of the cattle on the slopes; the vacher vociferating the Ranz des Vaches as he thinks of nothing in particular, and trims a stick with his pocket-knife; while all the time the 'brimming echoes spill the pleasant din' - these are the summer sounds which, though we should find it no easy matter to hear them in the towns without consulting the police, or, at any rate, writing to the papers, delight and intoxicate us in the Alps, and seem the only possible accompaniment for the magnificent glaciers and lovely flowers. Curious that so much discord should consort with such loveliness and yet not disturb it! Curious that so much discord should create such harmony! After all, dirt, as Lord Beaconsfield is said to have remarked, is only matter out of place; and here is discord quite at home. Untamed music amid untamed Nature, with net result - an entrancing harmony past imagining.

The Sulphur Anemone And Orchids At The Col De La Forclaz. In June.

It is a very different scene from that of spring. In spring these sounds would have struck an unreasonable note. Nature's awakening would have been too rude and noisy; there was a shy reserve about her wildness which it would never have done to so break in upon. But Summer's season is more flamboyant. Nature is in the fulness of life, and something of loudness is not out of tune. Vulgarity? No, that is not the right word. Summer in the Alps has nothing of vulgarity. Demureness, certainly, has vanished, but a great relative refinement remains. Summer's colours may be gaudy, her life may be demonstrative, but there is nothing in this that jars or hurts our sense of fitness. All things are in tune with the key-note of lustiness and vigour; all things are bent upon reaping a full harvest from the fierce sun, and are rightly alive with appropriate colour and gesture. Maybe this colour and gesture would be anything but aesthetic at another time and season, but now they speak of the very spirit of things -and speak most convincingly and sweetly. If these cow-bells were hushed, and did not wake us at dawn with their irresponsible chiming, we should feel that something was amiss; if the brightly-burnished little Copper butterflies were not flitting about the brilliant clear-yellow Dandelions, we should be sad; and it the vivid orange Arnica were not freely blooming amid a gorgeous wealth of rosy Rhododendron, we should think that things were out of joint. All is well! - the year is at its height, and nothing of this could we do without - nothing! No, not even the flies! We should indeed feel strange if the cattle-flies did not companion us! 'For sheer beauty and multiplicity of changing impression in colour, vegetation, composition of landscape scenery, the middle heights, before we quite leave the juicy pastures and forest foliage of the Alps (which means the pasturages), are the scenes of the most tranquil and continuous delight.' Thus writes Mr. Frederic Harrison; but he writes of days before those when 'Sings the Scythe to the flowers and grass.'

For the scythemen have been here, and the hay has been cut and gathered in from the pastures set apart for that purpose. If we were not here betimes, we have missed that wonderful point where Spring joins Summer in a riot of many colours; we have missed the undulating acres of mauve and rose, and white and gold, softened by the warm, grey, filmy sheen of flowering grasses. Two weeks or so ago these now 'stale, unprofitable' slopes and fields were a perfect marvel of varied tints. Here were broad masses of blue Campanula rkomboidalis blending with the rosy-mauve Crane's-bill (Geranium silvaticum), and with the lively pink Knottweed (Polygonum Bistorta) and the graceful pink-flowered Umbellifer (Pimpinella magna), forming a colour-scheme of most exquisite refinement. In the adjoining enclosure the scheme was more daring, for here masses of bright rose-pink Campion were strewn with the rich blue Knapweed (Cen-tanrea montana), with the rosy-white Masterwort (Astrantia major) and the gay yellow Globe-Flower; while more daring still were the slopes farther on, gorgeous with orange Arnica, red Knapweed (Centaurea uniflora), golden-brown Dandelion (Crepis aurea), yellow St. John's-Wort, and a host of blue Campanula, and pink, red, and mauve Orchids.

But all this has gone - cut by the scythe to make winter fodder for the cows. The neighbourhood now is in possession of the cattle and their attendant hordes of flies, seeking all they may devour! We must go farther afield; farther up to yet higher pastures, or to the stony slopes and the rough beds and sides of the mountain streams and glacier torrents. There we shall yet find 'A world with summer radiance drest' a world with 'Nature's ev'ry fair device, Mingled in a scented hoard.'

Nor should we delay. The cows will soon be moving higher, browsing and trampling things beyond this year's repair; but more especially will the goats - those omnivorous feeders, as far as vegetable life is concerned - be nibbling irreverently at shrub and grass and flower alike, clearing their district so that it looks as if a swarm of locusts had passed that way. Over on yonder Col we shall find Summer's Alpine splendours as yet undisturbed. Let us go.

Hood's lines are ringing in our ears:

'It was the time of roses - We plucked them as we passed!' for various Briars are in fullest beauty all along the path to the forest through which we must ascend. What a wonderful range of red and rosy colour! First and foremost is the dwarf and dainty Alpine Eglantine (Rosa alpina), of vivid magenta red, single blossom: a Rose belying the proverb about thorns. It is surprising that the Germans, generally so precise, should give the name of 'Alpenrose' to the Rhododendron, when this Eglantine exists as so distinctive, exquisite, and dazzling a feature of the Alpine flora. Mere beauty is not its only grace: a very wholesome and refreshing tea is made from the seed of this rose - a tea which is drunk by many vegetarians. Spreading bushes of Rosa pomifera are also here, with their abundance of fiery salmon or intense pink flowers harmonizing so admirably with their warm, blue-green foliage. And besides these two distinct roses there are many intermediate forms, their blossoms varying from shell-pink to white. Indeed, there are some which look uncommonly like our old friend the pale or blushing Dog Rose. The Genus is not an easy one to classify, there being so many forms which link up the varieties.

Rose-pink takes no second place to sky-blue in human esteem. Of all colours, pink - the pink of health, of life, and of perfection - makes perhaps the strongest appeal; and the very natural inclination is for us to linger over such a wondrous series of the freshest pinks as now surrounds us. Nor does this glow of health's own colour find its limits in the Roses. On the disintegrating sides of the rocks to our left is a great quantity of two very lovely Dianthus, Dianthus deltoides, and D). carthusian-orum, the pale blush of the former's large, single blossoms throwing the fiery little clustered flowers of the latter into striking relief. With these Rock-Pinks added to the Roses, harmonious gaiety could go no farther! And the grey-leaved Absinthe - the plant which is in such profusion beneath the Rose-bushes - is just the very setting for this pink and rosy glory. It is an aesthetic and a tuneful blend of colour, which even the most ultra upholder of 'the law against Absinthe' must admire, and admire aboundingly.

We must now scramble up this slope, where stands a waving group of the lovely lilac-plumed Thalictrum, as it were better to avoid passing too close to that cowshed ahead of us. We are not lonely. Many an innocent tourist will call inquisitively at the first cowshed he comes to, and so collect a horde of flies which will not leave his person until sundown - unless he stays his progress during the day, and of set and determined purpose slays them nimbly one by one. We will be wise in our generation, and take this short-cut! There is something really terrible in the persistence of a fly, and when, instead of one, there are sixty or a hundred flies - great iridescent, green-eyed creatures of stealthy habits, making their presence known only when they have dug their proboscis deep into the flesh - the persistence easily becomes maddening! No wonder the cattle will often stampede madly about the mountain-side, driven frantic by this terrible persistence! No wonder that it is often thought kinder to confine the cows to their sheds until sundown, when 'the wicked cease from troubling'!

There is comparatively little of interest in the forest through which we are now passing. Here and there, by the side of our path, and where there is more or less a break in the trees, are a few of that graceful little Masterwort, Astrantia minor, in company with a few plants of Saxifraga rotundi-folia and the yellow Wolfs-bane, or Monkshood (Acordtum Lycoctonum). Occasionally at the base of a pine there is some specimen of Broom-rape, or Orobanche, that curious Orchid-like group of plants which have, it is conjectured, turned parasitic, living on the roots of other plants, their own green leaves having thereby degenerated into dingy-brown scales. Here and there, too, stands in the semi-shade a stately group of the great creamy-plumed Spircea Aruncus, crept up from the valley below. This is La Reine des Bois; and certainly she is Queen of her race in Europe, if not elsewhere. As slowly we arrive above the forest limit, the Rhododendron bushes, laden with blossom, become more numerous, until, the last gnarled and stunted pine being left behind, we find ourselves in the midst of rosy-red acres, bordered with blue Gentian and flecked with orange Arnica - a unique and wonderful sight: Alpine summer in its boldest, most becoming robe. Our path is now winding gently upwards, making for the Col on the sky-line in front of us. We are passing along slopes running sharply down into a deep, rocky, forbidding-looking gorge cut by Spring's torrents from the snow on the Col and flanking peaks. And these slopes are densely clothed with Rhododendron (as Gorse will sometimes clothe our English downs and commons) in fullest blossom, bright rosy-red, sometimes palest pink, and - but this is far from common - sometimes white. Here and there between the bushes is the brilliant orange Arnica montana, the rich red - brown Gentiana purpurea, and occasionally this latter's near relative, the pale greenish-yellow Gentiana punctata. Here and there, too, is the vivid orange-red 'Grimm the Collier' (Hieracium aurantiacum) and the graceful Wintergreen (Pyrola minor), so like a robust blush-tinted Lily-of-the-Valley. Of Orchids there is a goodly number. The small white Coeloglossum albidum; Orchis globosa, with its distinctive lilac turban of blossom; the curious green and brown Frog Orchis (Orchis viridis); the rich brown-red Vanilla Orchid (Nigiitella angusti-f'olia); the Fragrant Orchid (Gymnadenia conopea); and last, but by no means least, the familiar and always welcome Night-scented or Butterfly Orchis (Habernaria bifolia), the 'sweet satyrian with the white flower' of Bacon - or is it Shakespeare ! - in his essay 'Of Gardens.'

Trollius Europaeus (The Globe Flower) And Geranium At The Col De La Forclaz, In June.

Strange to find this latter Orchid consorting with Rhododendron in the Swiss Alps! When last we met it was on the Surrey Downs! But 'sweet satyrian' is not the only feature here which carries our thoughts to England. There are the '. . . chequered butterflies, Like beams of Orient skies.'

Look yonder at that clear-yellow one skipping so briskly over the bushes: it has all the gay allure of the British Pale Clouded-Yellow, of which it must be no very distant cousin. It is Colias Palceno, whose food-plant is the Rhododendron. Its presence is reminiscent of English clover-fields - especially now that a really familiar member of the family, the Dark Clouded-Yellow, comes racing by. Palceno is a very beautiful insect. There is something so broad and pure about its design and colouring. Beautiful as is Edusa, the Dark Clouded-Yellow, or as is Hyale, the Pale Clouded-Yellow, this, their relative, at once strikes us as of greater, simpler refinement - refinement altogether in keeping with Alpine circumstance. Following the rule for insects, the female is more modestly apparelled; but, although she is paler, she is charming - fit consort for her black and citron-coloured lord. Then, again, that bright little chestnut-coloured insect, with thin black markings, flitting so swiftly from Dandelion to Dandelion, is Argynnis Pales, blood-relation of our small Fritillaries. Those Browns, too, playing about among the stones and grasses, are close connections of our Meadow Brown. And there, gambolling in the air, are two bright Blues, which at first sight it is pardonable to mistake for our Large Blue (Lyccena Avion); this, however, is Lycaena Damon, a near relation, though a stranger to English soil. They have settled now on yonder plants of Thyme; and there beside them, deeply absorbed in the sweet blossoms, are one or two brilliant Alpine Coppers (Polyommatus Vergaureae), obviously allied to the Great Copper now extinct in England, but likely, let us hope, to be restored by the good offices of Wicken Fen. A brilliant specimen of the Swallowtail, too, is coming up the slope in rapid, tumbled flight. This insect (Papilio Machaon - another British butterfly likely to benefit by the establishment of Wicken Fen as a preserve) is common throughout Switzerland, straying much higher up into the Alps than the Scarce Swallow-tail (P. Podalirius), though this latter is plentiful along some of the hot and dusty roads of the plains. The absence of Podalirius upon the Alps is due to its conservative taste in food, the Blackthorn and the Sloe ceasing at about 2,000 feet; whereas the Common Swallow-tail adapts its appetite to Alpine food-stuff, and feeds willingly on several of the mountain Umbelliferae.

But here we are, at the base of the steeper slopes mounting to the Col. We had best leave the path, though it follow an easier gradient; for, by ascending direct, we shall see more of the flowers. We have now left the zone of Rhododendron, and have gone one good step nearer the elite of Alpine things. Here, nestling in the close turf, is the little mauve-flowered Gentiana tenella, growing with that other annual Gentian, the exquisite little bright blue G. nivalis, together with a few plants of its far more local mauve form, said by some to be a distinct variety. And here is a plant of its white form growing close to this colony of G. campestris. Here, also, is the white Alpine Butterwort, or Catchfly (Pinguicula alpina), a member of the vegetation which is far from being a vegetarian! And here, in the hollow, by this patch of melting snow, is the frail little Snowbell (Soldanella pusilla), much smaller than our old friend S. alpina, though bearing an unmistakable likeness to its more ubiquitous relative. And here is yet another link with England and some of the copses of Essex and Cambridgeshire - Primula elatior, the Oxlip! Really, the invasion of the Swiss Alps by the British seems not to be confined to any one creation! What with the Stinging-Nettle, the Yellow Colt's-foot, the 'sweet satyrian,' the Oxlip, and that Cabbage-White Butterfly fluttering up the slope over there, the invasion appears as much vegetable and insect as human!

Once again, then, we catch a glimpse of the difficulty, and even, strictly speaking, the impossibility of drawing sharp, dogmatic lines anywhere in circumstance. The so-called hard-and-fast principle of 'each country for its countrymen' is merely the relative principle of a season. Men may raise and maintain vast fleets and armies for the protection and imposition of this principle, but the inevitable trend of things is towards 'share and share alike.' Men may attempt to resist this trend of things - they may make all strenuous efforts to negative it - but in the end their efforts are so many efforts in its favour. The trend is, in spite of all, for nation to absorb nation. And are there no indications of this trend in other creations than Man? May it not be that the goal of brotherhood is not for him alone? May it not be that evolution is diminishing disabilities and extending adaptability in other directions besides that of the human species? Have we to suppose that, apart from Man, the last word upon the tendency to relative ubiquity is expressed to-day by the Horse, the Sparrow, the House-fly, or the Nettle? There is much temptation to think that we have not; there seems much to indicate that Man has no monopoly of the tourist spirit, precursor of settlement. A not altogether pleasing prospect this, contemplating it through present-day-glasses. Beauty - as we now understand it - must suffer if Brotherhood is to gain, for variety must, obviously, be suppressed to a large extent. And, with us of to-day, 'variety is charming,' and is, indeed, of the very salt of life.

But we are out for a little mild botany, not for cloudy philosophy! Our excuse must be that our surroundings provoke such reflections. There is so little here of the hustle and bustle of the world, or, at any rate, of civilization. All around us Nature seems so placid. Speaking vaguely, 'the things that matter in life' are, for the nonce, far-distant, and the temptation is to lapse into abstractions. Our wayward speculations have, in any case, carried us over the ground, for here we are on the Col! Orthodoxy would have us expatiate upon the view, which is superb, truly superb, vibrating as it is with those actinic rays so belauded of photographers, so beloved of Alpine flowers; but we are bent more upon the vegetable details of the immediate foreground - and (oh, exceptional incident!) we have with us no Kodak! What is that field of silvery, shimmering white just below us, where the sparkling little stream is overflowing its usual course? It must be Cotton-Grass; not the common Cotton-Grass with pendant white tassels, but Eriophorum Scheuchzeri, sometimes known as the Hare's-tail Rush, with one large, erect, silky, white plume - an ideal thing of which to gather a quantity for the winter decoration of our vases. When it is seen growing, as is not infrequently the case, with quantities of the laughing-blue Bavarian Gentian, the harmonious delight of colour is such as is verily 'fit food for the gods'! Gentiana bavarica, like many another water-loving

Alpine, is not a marsh plant, as is the Cotton-Grass; when this Gentian associates with the Cotton-Grass, it is always upon the drier, more substantial spots amid the marshy ground. Those who see such plants growing in moist ground, and who wish to succeed with them in their gardens at home, should remember that throughout the long winter months here in the Alps the ground is frozen hard and dry. Failure will dog all attempts to treat this Gentian (and many another Alpine which loves water during the summer) as a bog-plant in England.

Now, bearing to the right, we will follow along the slopes which lead to the turfy shoulder of the peak on the opposite side of the gorge to that by which we ascended. There is much the same flora on these slopes as on the last steep slopes before we reached the Col, except that here, on this stony shelf over which we are passing, is a quantity of the always fascinating little trailing Alpine, Linaria alpina, or Alpine Toad-Flax, with its charming mauve and orange blossoms and cool, grey-green foliage. There exists a variety which has no orange lips, but it is very much more local, and is not growing here; nor is its extremely uncommon pink form, reported as having been recently found in the neighbourhood of Bourg St. Pierre. This Toad-Flax is obviously a member of the family of Snapdragon, and its blossom bears a strong likeness to the Mother-of-Thousands or Wandering Sailor (Linaria cymbalaria) of our English walls. The popular family name of Toad-Flax is said to be derived from the common yellow Snapdragon of the plains, whose appearance, before flowering, resembles a many-leaved plant of Flax, and the mouth of whose yellow blossom is supposed to resemble that of a Toad.

Having reached the shoulder at which we were aiming, we shall now have to turn straight down its northern side - down into this amphitheatre of rugged cliffs. And here the nature of the ground is entirely different. Crumbled rock takes the place of turf, and huge boulders lie strewn about the steep declivity. Snow, too, still fills many of the gullies. With such a change in aspect and condition there is bound to be a change in vegetation, and we shall find few of the things which people the sunny, grassy slopes we are leaving behind us. Sure enough, here is a widespread colony of an Alpine

Crowfoot (Ranunculus glacialis), with its shining white flowers, which rapidly turn a madder red after the bees, flies, or winds have visited them - much in the manner of the Box-leaved Polygala, of Micheli's Daisy, and of Lathyrus luteus. The Alpine Toad-Flax is here, too, in profusion; and an Alpine Willow-herb (Epilobium Fleischeri), with its rosy flowers and cottony seed; so, also, is that brilliant and arresting gem, Sempervivum arachnoideum, with its bright brick-red or crimson stars enlivening the severe, grey rock. Several Saxifrages are also here: the violet-red Saxifraga oppositifolia. the greenish-yellow S. muscoides, and the cream - coloured S. aspera, with golden yellow at the base of each petal; while on these sunnier rocks is many a rosette of S. Aizoon, the commonest and yet one of the loveliest of Swiss Saxifrages, and varying greatly as regards the red spots on its creamy-white flowers. Here, also, in the dripping moss on these reeking rocks, is the Yellow Mountain Saxifrage (S. aizoides), together with its bright chestnut-coloured form (S. atrorubens). And what a wonderful sight is the Forget-me-not (Myosotis alpestris), as it springs in bright profusion from the grey-green stones! Some there are who regard this Myosotis as but an Alpine form of the Wood Forget-me-not (M. sylvatica); but however that may be, Forget-me-not reigns here as it reigns below, captivating the heart and mind of everyone who sees it - and this, too, in spite of all its many rivals for our praises and attention. The Forget-me-not of the plains, much as we admire its cool, clear blue, never reaches the intensity of colour of its Alpine kinsman; and in the brilliant green moss growing around this small water-course the Forget-me-not is boldly mingling with immense quantities of the brilliant blue Gentiana bavarica, of deeper, richer, more summery blue than verna. None but Nature could have blended so harmoniously these two blues as they are here. Is it the green of the moss that makes the blend so possible, so acceptable? Dressmakers say they can harmonize any two seemingly antagonistic tints or colours by putting a break of black between. Possibly Nature uses green to a like end and purpose. In any case, nothing in the way of colour-harmony seems to affright her; she dares all, and dares without fault or failure.

Alpine Garden (La Rambertia) On The Rochers De Naye, Above Montreux. At The End Of June. With The Jungfrau, Eiger, And Monch In The Distance.

We must now make for that farther green Col, across this slope of thick Heather and Sphagnum; then we shall come in sight of our starting-point down below, for we are working round in almost a circle. Except for a few of the pale porcelain-blue Campanula barbata, and an occasional specimen of its white-blossomed form, there are few flowers here. This slope will be perfect in Autumn, when the Heather is out. For the moment we are granted a pause in the feast of colour: one of those healthy interludes so necessary for the repose of attention and the avoidance of a sated interest. But, evidently, fresh attractions are ahead of us. These gay butterflies, complements of the flowers, are not speeding for nothing in such hot haste across this grey-green waste.

We are once again in flowerland; we are arrived upon this second Col! Small wonder that the butterflies were in such a hurry! The slaty, ungenerous-looking ground to our left, covered sparsely with a reticent growth of grass, is a veritable garden. Here is a wellnigh infinite profusion of Aster alpinus, whose blue-mauve flowers (here and there pink, or even white), with golden centres, harmonize so admirably with the host of dark wine-red heads of the sweet-smelling Vanilla Orchid, and with the pale canary-yellow of the Alyssum, or

Mountain Madwort Here, also, are several late patches of Gentiana brachyphylla, a close relation of G. verna Alche-milla is nestling, green - flowered, everywhere. Although insignificant of blossom, this is a plant it would be hard to part with from the Alps; moreover, and as Lord Avebury points out in his 'Beauties of Nature,' its properties form an essential part of the finest Gruyere cheeses. Skipping light-heartedly amongst the Asters is a true Alpine butterfly which we have not noticed before - Melitoea Cynthia, one of the most distinctive of the Fritillaries, with wings of a dark blue-purple, flecked with white and russet: an insect whose season of beauty, like that of the Rhododendron-loving Colias, is short, owing to the high winds which sweep the localities in which it is generally found. To secure good specimens, it is well to be up in its haunts (the neighbourhood of the Col de Balme, for instance) about the second week in July. Above us, to the left, under the lichen-scarred rocks and amongst the fallen debris, we can espy several groups of the scarce Alpine Poppy, smaller and more delicate than that favourite of our gardens, the Iceland Poppy; like this latter, it varies in colour - white, pink, orange, or yellow - but only the white form is growing hereabouts. And what a curious grass this is (Poa alpina; forma vivipara) amongst which all these flowers are growing! It is possessed of a novel method of propagation. Looking closely, what at first appears to be the usual flower-head is seen to be really a plume of small plants, already showing tiny roots. The increasing weight of these progeny as they develop bears the plume to the ground, and there they take root around their parent.

But we must be moving on; the first tints of sunset are already touching the snow and ice on yonder glacier, and 'Darker grows the valley, more and more forgetting.'

As we descend the sheltered slope to reach the pastures where are the cattle - and the flies! - we come across a host of Bell-Gentian. This is Gentiana acaulis, known vulgarly in our gardens as Gentianella. Though much resembling Gentiana Kochiana, it is smaller, and has not on its throat the green rays of the latter; its dark green leaves, too, are hard and thick, whereas the leaves of Kochiana are dull-green and flabby. These two Gentians are commonly confounded, possibly because there appear to be intermediate forms. Indeed, a not unusual mistake amongst flower - lovers, and especially amongst gardeners, is to call all the Bell-Gentians by the one name, acaulis, thus including Gentiana Clusii, which is less marked with green than Kochiana, and has hard, pointed leaves, standing more erect; and also Gentiana alpina, with green rays, likewise, down the throat of the flower, but with short oval leaves of a yellowish-green. One is inclined to presume that the flora of the Alps has long ago been thoroughly mapped out, discussed, and determined; but such is not really the case. Relatively little there is, perhaps, which is final. In any case, much remains to be done in many directions, and there is still ample occasion for the scientific enthusiast to add lustre to his name. Botany is comparatively a young study - as, indeed, all such studies are young. We have no more heard 'the Last word' on the subject than we have discovered the last plant. 'One of the delights of the observation of live things,' says Mr. W. Beach Thomas, 'is that you are perpetually unlearning established truths,' and of few, if any, things is this more true than of plants, and of that all-round study of plants which Botany should mean.

But here we are at length at the first cow-chalet, and we may as well sit down awhile. We have been walking for nearly five hours, and have earned a meed of repose. Not that five hours' walking is any extraordinary feat in the Alps! With such pure, invigorating air, and so much to absorb attention, five hours pass as easily as, and with no more fatigue than, one hour will pass on a close and dusty high-road in the plains. The flies? No, no; we shall not now be bothered by the flies! Just before sunset is their bed-time, and at that hour they disappear as if by magic. We may sit down with perfect equanimity beside this ancient, storm-worn cross, where the little cow-boy is busily tying up blossoms of the purple Alpine Viola into bunches to dry for Winter use as tea for chills and colds.

How peaceful is the glorious panorama: true type, in every way, of the bright, seductive side of Alpine circumstance!, On yonder tall Alpine Thistle the lovely Apollo butterfly has already closed its vermilion-eyed wings in sleep; from yonder cowshed musically troop the cows, after some hours of comparative seclusion from their enemies, the flies; in yonder rose-blue sky circles a black, dot-like Eagle, searching the landscape for his evening's meal; up yonder mountains creep the purple shades of sundown, invading more and more the bright, ruddy gold of the sunlit cliffs and crags; while everywhere there reigns 'A glister over all the air, A glister as of diamond wine; A dazzled ether shrinking in the shine.'

Truly a scene to ponder over; fit conclusion to a full, round day of fascination! Some there are who will surely dub our day a day of tame performance; will cavil at our want of proper zeal; will say we had shown a more appropriate spirit had we treated with the mountains as zestful climbers should, scaling their topmost peaks away above the last poor weed. Well, well! it is good there should be other views to hand besides our own:

'To him who in the love of Nature holds Communion with her visible forms, she speaks A various language.'

Alpine Garden (La Rambertia) At The Summit Of The Rochers De Naye, In The Clouds At The End Of June.

CHAPTER VII. CONCERNING SOME SPRING AND SUMMER ALPINES

It is probably safe to say that every manifestation of Beauty can claim its victims. Certain it is that Beauty, as represented by Alpine flowers, can make such claim and rank it high. In spite of all warning precedent, each year lengthens the roll of victims to this one of Beauty's forms; each year the Alpine flora lures the unwary and immoderate to mishap and disaster. Beauty is inoffensive - ay, it is more than inoffensive, it is beneficent - always providing, however, that we do not try to gather too much of it to ourselves. In itself, it can never so belie its name as to be disastrous. 'Beauty unadorned' is flawless; the mischief is in ourselves - blind, eager, immoderate, indiscreet - and all that we put upon our ideal. And when, as in the case of the Edelweiss, Beauty is linked with Tradition, our immoderation is apt to be the more pressing and inevitable, and Beauty receives a value and notoriety it should never possess.

But the pursuit of floral beauty - the pursuit of Botany, or the mere dilettante enthusiasm for plucking desirable flowers - in the Alps is not necessarily rash and dangerous. Danger exists anywhere the moment we act dangerously, and it is a mistake to think that we must necessarily risk broken bones, or perhaps our lives, in order to gather Edelweiss. The popular atmosphere surrounding this plant is charged with a goodly percentage of exaggeration. It is not rare for people fresh to Switzerland to pay her their first visit with brains obsessed by strange, weird myths and notions of Edelweiss and all things Alpine. Even in the plains, a simple Rhubarb-tart is made of Alpine Rhubarb, and is relished accordingly with untold ecstasy; and when the immediate region of the Alps is reached, and eyes peer out through the distorting hazes of Tradition, mere Marguerites have been known to take on the face and form of Edelweiss!

Edelweiss does, of course, grow often in sheer, precipitous places, but it is also often to be found within quite easy reach, and where there is no shadow of danger to life or limb. On one occasion (before the forts monopolized the superb rock of Dailly) I watched for over an hour, through binoculars, a peasant gathering Edelweiss on the hot, precipitous cliffs of the Dent de Morcles. He had been there, I was told, since early morning, worming his way along the narrow ledges, his only hold being some tuft of grass or crevice in the rock. He looked like a fly on a wall, and it was preposterous to think that he should be thus risking his life for the few pence which these flowers would bring him from the visitors at the hotel. Yet so it was. Towards evening he arrived, a worn but sturdy montagnard, quite oblivious of having accomplished anything which could be considered unusual, and glad to sell for a matter of fifteen pence all that might easily have cost him so much more dear. And only across the valley, on the sides of the Dent du Midi, I could have taken him to a spot where he might have gathered thrice the quantity in half an hour, and at no personal risk whatever. His exploit, however, went far to confirm and swell the popular romance surrounding this Alpine.

Known sometimes as Silverstar, and in French as Belle Étoile, or Étoile d' Argent, Leontopodium alpinum, the far-famed Edelweiss, is by no means rare. Nor is it distinctive of the Swiss Alps. Although absent in the Arctic regions, it is common in Siberia, Japan, New Zealand, China, and on the Himalayas; and it is a bridal flower in Austria, Hungary, and the Tyrol. In Switzerland itself it is common, especially on limestone formation; there are places where it is abundant on the Alpine pastures, and is mown down by the scythe, or eaten with avidity by the cows. But its range of altitude is not a wide one. Mr. H. Stuart Thompson, who has made a special study of the altitudinal limits of Alpine plants, gives the limit for Edelweiss in the Western Alps as 8,200 feet; and others give its range in the Alps generally as from about 5,700 feet to some 8,700 feet. On this score, then, there are flowers of more Alpine habit than this plant of swollen reputation - flowers such as the exquisitely lovely little blue Eritrichium nanum, the Mousse d'azur. And on the score of beauty, the 'blossom' of the Edelweiss is more curious than beautiful. 'That which looks,' says Dr. C. Schroter, 'like a large flower at the end of the stalk is in reality a very composite structure. It consists of numerous many-flowered heads, whose white, woolly, radially-arranged bracts imitate a flower.' This peculiarity can be better seen in a Japanese relative, Leontopodium Japonicum, a species with the lower leaves green, resembling the leaves of a shrubby Veronica, and those around the insignificant flower-head a powdery white.

We shall perhaps be forgiven, then, if we find it a little strange that the Edelweiss should have so inflamed the imagination of the world, and should have become so obsessing an emblem of the Swiss Alps. Its title seems scarcely to fit the facts; indeed, face to face with these, it appears not a little monstrous. Maybe the bridal tradition has much to do with the flower's enormous repute. Its halo is evidently of no recent date. In a fifteenth-century portrait of a Swiss lady a bunch of this flower is being carried in the hand; and in some parts of Switzerland to-day a bouquet of Edelweiss and Vanilla Orchid handed to a girl by a man stands for a proposal of marriage. Maybe, too - and this, no doubt, is a still more potent factor - the deaths which the plant has occasioned have helped to place it as high as it is upon the scroll of fame: for the price we pay is so often the reason and measure for our esteem.

Now, that other 'everlasting,' the dainty little rose and white Antennaria dioica (Gnaphalium dioicum, Linn.), is really quite as fascinating as, and assuredly prettier than, the Edelweiss. True, it is commoner, far commoner, and it does not affect awesome cliffs and precipices - although, no doubt, it may at times be found so situated that the gathering of it would, for those who wish, entail some risk. And in a humbler, less noisy-way it is popular - if nomenclature is any test of popularity - for it is known variously as Mountain Cudweed, Chast weed, Mountain Everlasting, Cat's-ear, and Cat's-paw. It has, too, variety of blossom in its favour. On the male plant the flowers are round, and on the female they are long; while the range of colour in both male and female runs from white, through pink, to a deep rose. I know of few things more charming in this regard than a bouquet of this little flower in all its various tints. And if the Edelweiss is beloved of sheep and chamois, well, so also is the Mountain Cudweed, with its soft, woolly leaves; moreover, it is used most readily by the peasants for the making of an effective cough-mixture.

But the Mountain Cudweed cannot pretend to be purely and simply an Alpine; although it is found up to about 8,500 feet on wellnigh every mountain, it is common in the plains. There is, however, an Alpine 'everlasting' which might reasonably oust the Edelweiss from some of its pride of place. This is Eryngium alpinum, the popular Chardon Bleu of the Swiss, Panicaut or Reine de l' Alpe of the French, and Blue Thistle of the English. It is not a common plant by any means, seeking refuge, as it seems to do, in very out-of-the-way places. Like the chamois, it is known to most only by repute, or from captive specimens, alive or dead. Nor is its distribution in Switzerland a wide one; it is said not to be found at all in the Canton of Valais. Unfortunately, it is one of the plants which has suffered most severely at the hands of the vandal uprooter, and more than once I have seen peasants hawking the roots amongst the hotels of a mountain resort. There is a spot, not a hundred miles from Montreux, where this distinguished flower can be found in comparative abundance, growing amid the Rhododendron-bushes; but the area is a restricted one, and north, south, east and west of it may be searched and drawn blank. The popularity of the plant is such that many a chalet's plot of ground will possess it, though possessing no other flower. I remember once returning from the mountains to the plains with several bunches of this Blue Thistle, which, before reaching home, had been reduced to but part of one bunch. In the train and on the steamer people (all of them Swiss) begged and prayed for 'just one bloom,' and it was only by a tardy show of firmness that a few blooms remained to myself.

Unlike the popularity of the Edelweiss, that of the Blue Thistle, as far as I know, owes little to the risk and danger of seeking it where it grows; it is comparatively rare that it shows a liking for cliff and precipice. If it has its tale of woe, it is less decided than that of another and very lovely flower, Aquilegia alpina. Growing often in 'ugly' places, this exquisite and far from common bright blue Columbine has been more than once known to cause disaster. And the same may be said for the yellow Alpine Auricula (Primula auricula). In fact, the same could doubtless be said of many another plant: for variety in the circumstance of each flower is not wanting in the Alps, and thus there is no lack of suitable opportunity for the foolish or foolhardy to indulge in freak performances.

While on the question of risk and danger attaching to Alpines, mention may perhaps be made of several which are dangerous on account of their poisonous properties. The stately blue Monk's-hood (Aconitum napellus), for instance, bears the label 'Dangerous.' Here is beauty capable of inflicting a very different kind of mischief from the Edelweiss; yet, if treated with discernment, its properties are nothing but beneficent. It is much used in homoeopathy. One of the last of Summer's flowers, it frequents pastures and shrubby slopes from about 1,500 feet to some 6,000 feet in districts frequented by the Humble-bee, which insect, apparently, is this flower's only faithful friend and aid to fertilization. A curious fact about this plant is that, although the cattle will not touch it as it grows, they eat it, and eat it with impunity, in the dry hay. A. Lycoctonum is its less civilized, less erect-growing, yellow-flowered brother, its popular name of Yellow Wolfs-bane (more expressive in French as Tue-loup) warning us of the family aptitude if treated injudiciously!

Alpines On The Cloud-Swept Limestone Rocks Of The Rochers De Naye, With The Mountains Of Gruyere In The Background, At The Beginning Of July.

Perhaps the most used, medicinally, of all poisonous Alpine plants is the large orange-flowered Arnica (Arnica montana). Found at from about 3,000 feet to about 6,000 feet, its roots, leaves, and flowers (especially its flowers) are used to make a tincture for the treatment of cuts, bruises, and rheumatism. The peasant sometimes smokes its leaves by way of tobacco (in France it is known as Tabac des Savoyards) - however, the peasant is not usually fastidious as regards the 'weed' he smokes! The cows commonly avoid this Arnica - though I know of no evidence that it is injurious to them. This is more than can be said of another striking mountain plant, Veratrum album. This the cattle have excellent reason for not touching: it is intensely poisonous. With its large, deeply-ridged, dark green leaves and tall spike of greenish-yellow flowers, it is a handsome feature of damp pastures. Tourists frequently mistake it for the tall and stately Yellow Gentian (Gentiana lutea), with which it is often found growing, and to which, in the earlier stages of its growth, it bears some resemblance. But the Yellow Gentian has more oval leaves, of a lighter green, and different texture. If the cows eat of this Gentian the milk acquires a very bitter taste, and is spoilt. In its proper place, however, this bitter taste is much appreciated by the Swiss. The celebrated Gentian-Bitter, excellent for indigestion, is made from the long, yellow, deep-growing root, and guides use it as a warming and invigorating cordial at high altitudes.

An Alpine of the fullest grace and fascination is Thalictrum aquilegifolium, growing airy-light among the formal Rhododendron or other bushes on some semi-shaded slope, its slender flower-stem crowned with a mauve or creamy-white, cloud-like plume of stamen. A blood-relation, T. adiantifolium, is a sacred plant in China, and it would scarcely occasion any great surprise were some such reverence shown in Switzerland to its Alpine brother. Moreover, to use a well-worn phrase - one which breathes, perhaps, no very high philosophy - it is useful as well as beautiful. From its root is extracted a yellow dye, also a medicine employed in cases of jaundice and intermittent fever. Nor ought we to overlook the usefulness of the Rhododendron amongst which this lovely Meadowrue so frequently grows; for both its leaves and its flowers are effectively used against rheumatism - and more or less successfully (according to taste) as an ingredient of Swiss tea!

Did space permit, this list could be extended to four or five times its length: for it is astonishing the number of Alpines which are of economic use. Living as close as he does to Nature, the montagnard of the Swiss Alps knows in remarkable degree the properties of his Alpine flora. Viola calcarata, Adonis vernalis, Saponaria ocymoides, Trifolium alpinum, Petasites niveus, Gentiana germanica, several of the Ferns and Orchids, and many other plants, are carefully sought out and harvested by the provident peasant. But much as there is still that might be said, we cannot linger. This present work makes no pretence of being a complete manual of any kind or sort. Needs must that we should pass on now to the flowers of Alpine Autumn.

CHAPTER VIII. AUTUMN IN THE ALPS

'Hear ye no sound of sobbing in the air V The poetic pessimist is usually rampant at this season. With long face and moist eye he sighs of 'the ah-ness of things,' declares that 'in my heart is grief,' and looks upon Nature as passing to the tomb, meet subject for depression and tears. He is the same, probably, who sang with such inordinate optimism in the Spring; for extremes do ever tend to meet. Driven to a desperate optimism by the wearying gloom of a blank, Winter-inspired pessimism, he sang exuberantly of vernal promise, of Summer's heated splendour; and now here he is, back once again in the depths of melancholy, having travelled - always in the same extravagantly ornate yet dilapidated conveyance - the year's cycle of extreme emotion. For him Autumn is cause for despondency and the wringing of hands. For him the mountains are sombre and forbidding, the weather fitful and wild, the bright fruits and berries but a sign of decadence, and Nature generally in a bad, depressing way. All things are putting on a dress of mourning, and it is only decent, he avers, that thoughts should be of death and of the grave. To be sure, he may address to Autumn some such words as did Keats:

'Where are the songs of Spring? Ay, where are they? Think not of them, thou hast thy music too;' but what a terribly doleful music our pessimist makes of it! And yet the music of Autumn is not the wailing dirge he would have us to understand; there is strength in it, promise in it, life in it. Autumn has no lack of gladness; but 'l' oeil qui pleure trop finit par s'aveugler,' and our poet's eyes are blinded by his pessimistic tears. Who was it wrote:

'It ain't no good to grumble and complain; It's easier and cheaper to rejoice. When God serves out the weather, and sends rain, Well - rain's my choice!'?

Whoever it was, he was a well-regulated optimist, one more likely to catch the real beauty, the true music of things. Ruskin said much the same in speaking of the king of Welsh mountains: 'God never sent bad weather to Snowdon yet - only variations of good.' And that is the spirit in which Autumn in the Alps should be greeted. There should be 'No sense of aught but of her loveliness.'

Blended with its own strong individuality there is a distinct strain of Spring, a marked note of promise, in an Alpine Autumn. Nature is not dour and hopeless. A rainbow-coloured arc domes the season - an arc in which the hopeful tints of Spring are prominently present. Bright and tender blue is there, in the two autumnal Gentians and in the reappearing Vernal Gentian; so also are the clear and tender greens and yellows, in the changing foliage of the Alpine Eglantine, the Alpine Honeysuckles, and many another deciduous bush and shrub; whilst red - as strong and vigorous a red as at any time of year - pervades the whole with a full and ample note of life. It might be thought that with, on every hand, such broad, dense forests of 'Green pine, unchanging as the days go by, an autumnal glory of foliage would be most noticeable by its absence. But this is not the case. The Alps glow with colour, and the sombre Pines and Rhododendrons do but serve as admirable, enhancing contrasts. See how, below us on the slopes, the mountain Cherry-trees are afire with brilliant crimson-lake and cadmium; look over at the wine-red haze of Bilberry which pervades yonder expanse of Rhododendron; or at the flame-like patches of Geranium and other plants on yonder scree; mark, too, in these steep and stony places, the flaring profusion of Berberis, veritable ' burning bushes,' with their orange foliage and cascades of scarlet fruit; notice how the golden Larch sparkles amid ' the dark and secret pine,' and how, upon every rock and boulder, the plants, mosses, ferns, and lichens are aglow with rich yellows, reds, and browns. Yes, Autumn in the Alps can vie with Autumn elsewhere, and can ring out as gladsome a note as any note in Spring.

Nor by any means is the season lacking in charming flowers. On rough, shady slopes the graceful Willow Gentian {Gentiana asclepiadea), with its long sprays of pointed leaves and rich blue flowers (sometimes pure white), is the equal of anything to be found earlier in the year; as is that other autumnal Gentian, G. ciliata, the

Bearded Gentian, its lively, sun-loving flowers brightening the shaly banks by the side of the paths and roads.

Rhododendron And Thalictrum, And The Glacier De Trient. The Middle Of July.

In the neighbourhood of this latter Gentian will be 'The pliant harebell, swinging in the breeze On some grey rock;' not, however, the harebell of which Wordsworth sang, but the diminutive porcelain-blue (sometimes white) Campanula pusilla. Dianthus superbus, the Fringed Pink, doing full justice to its Latin name, can be found in semi-shade at the edge of copse or forest, and in company with the False Box (Polygala Chamoebuxus), aflower again as in the Spring; and late specimens of the stately brown-red, purple-spotted Martagon Lily are often found of this company. Gentiana verna, together very often with G. Kochiana, is making its reappearance, towards the end of September, in the parched turf - coming purposely, it would seem, to bid us a cheerful 'au revoir, and not good-bye.' The Monk's-hood and the Wolf's-bane, too, are in bloom well into the Autumn, as also are the two Masterworts (Astrantia major and minor) in some sheltered spot at the fringe of the forest. Tucked away among the lichened rocks, on which basks the lazy, agile lizard, two white or rosy little Catchflies (Silene rupestris and S. quadrifida) may still be found in flower, not far away from the white Alpine Mouse-ear (Cerastium alpinum), the Grass of Parnassus (Parnassia palustris) - more like a white Ranunculus than a grass! - and the creamy-white Saxi-fraga aspera and the yellow S. aizoides - all of them blooming comparatively freely for this late season, and often associating with dwarf and sturdy specimens of the poisonous, scarlet-berried shrub Daphne Mezereum, and with the russet or grey-black viper, sunning himself while yet he may, and announcing, probably, the approach of a storm.

Now that the cattle and the goats have moved lower down towards their winter quarters, many a plant that had its bloom-spike eaten off earlier in the year tries its best at this season to recover lost ground. In this way, on the pastures, Autumn will be wearing 'Late blooms of second childhood in his hair.'

Here we may often find, even to the end of October, such flowers as the two mauve, annual Gentians (Gentiana germanica and G. campestris), the Mountain Avens (Geum montanum), the grey-blue Bearded Bell-flower (Campanula barbata), and three of the dark blue or blue-purple Rampions (Phyteuma Michelli, P.hemisphaericum, and P.orbiculare). And the same late and hasty effort may be seen among the flowers in the hay-fields. Recovering from the effects of the scythe, such summer things as the Alpine Knapweed (Centaurea uniflora), with its cobwebby-looking buds and brilliant magenta - red blooms, the Wood Crane's - bill (Geranium sylvaticum), and Campanula rhomboid-alis, making a brave show amongst the profusion of Autumn Crocus (Colchicum autumnale). This lovely magenta-pink Crocus, although so common in the Alps, is not, strictly speaking, an Alpine. It has, however, its Alpine form in Colchicum alpinum, a smaller, daintier flower with a pale yellow stem - the stem of autumnale being white. Both of these bulbous plants (of which white forms may occasionally be found) are violently poisonous, and are injurious to the cattle. One hears them sometimes called by the name of Saffron; but the Saffron Crocus is C. sativus, cultivated in some parts of France, and probably of Oriental origin. Frequently in the Spring of the year people will ask the name of the lily-like plant with the large green 'bud' set deep among the leaves, and I have known some who have transplanted it to their gardens, and watched eagerly for the 'bud' to expand. They were, of course, doomed to disappointment, and it has been a case of the watched kettle never boiling! For the fact is, this was no flower-bud, but simply the unripe seed-pod. The habit of this Crocus is to bloom leafless in the Autumn, and then to hide its seed-vessel beneath the ground until the Spring, when it throws it up with its leaves to ripen. But this is only the habit of autumnale; alpinum ripens its seed at once, after flowering.

We cannot leave the Autumn flowers without some mention of that which is possibly the most characteristic of them all - the Carline or Stemless Thistle (Carlina acaulis). With its glistening, silvery flower-head set close to the ground, this plant, so effectively and unpleasantly on the defensive, is one of the most attractive features of the Alps at this season. Seeming to like all soils, it is abundant; but it is none the less attractive, and its bloom-heads are often cut and dried by the ladies wherewith to decorate their hats. The peasants look upon it as a weather-glass, for it closes at the approach of rain and storm. They eat the head, too, much as we do the heads of the Globe Artichoke; they also distil from it a tonic. Nor is the Carline Thistle unknown in the pages of History; an angel is said to have pointed out its medicinal properties to Charlemagne, who promptly took the hint, and so saved himself and his army from the plague.

If many lovely flowers are still with us, so also are many gay butterflies, disputing possession with the bees. Many of the Browns are flitting about the rocks and among the grasses and small, pale yellow Dandelions. The Clouded Yellow, several of the Skippers, and the Humming Bird and Bee Hawk moths seem as quick and as eager as ever; while three species at least of Blues and the Alpine Copper are still absorbed in the blossoms of the Thyme. Vanessa, too, are common - including that rare British insect, the Camberwell Beauty - sunning themselves on the rocks, roads, and paths, and expanding 'the painted rainbows on their wings.' And at sundown come the Sphinx moths, particularly the Pine and the Spurge Hawk, darting feverishly from flower to flower.

Then there are those flowers of the forest, the Fungi. If climatic conditions have been favourable, the display of these is astonishingly rich and brilliant, changing the otherwise gloomy forests into veritable gardens of colour. Scarlet, rose, purple, mauve, orange, blue-green, white, and yellow, they are of almost infinite variety in form and tint, and come as a revelation to those who, hitherto, have known only the mushroom and one or two brown toadstools. But the season's riot of conspicuous colour is due in large measure to the profusion of wild fruits and berries. Mention has already been made of the fiery robe with which the Berberis (Berberis vulgaris) clothes itself. A thickly-fruited group of this graceful shrub growing in some rocky ravine is a truly arresting sight. The Swiss make an excellent jam and jelly from the fruit, and confectioners use it for colouring sweets. No stranger to England (it is to be found, for instance, in Shakespeare's County, on the banks of the Avon), the wood was at one time employed by tanners, and it is said that the Ancient Britons extracted from it a yellow dye, with which they were wont to stain and beautify their savage persons. Another of the season's fiery bushes is the Mountain or Grape Elder (Sambucus racemosa), with its bunches of closely-packed, coral-red berries. In spite of all superficial appearances to the contrary, this is a member of the Honeysuckle family, and more than often it associates with two of the shrubby Honeysuckles - Lonicera alpigena, with red, cherry-like berries, and L. nigra, bearing black, twin berries. Then there is the Holly Thorn (Cotoneaster vulgaris), with small, violet-red fruit; Sorbus aria, with white backs to its leaves and clusters of scarlet fruit, which are edible; the Alpine Juniper (Juniperus nana), with purple-blue berries, from which a kind of gin is made; the various Eglantines, with their showy red fruit, some round and shining, some large and hairy (Rosa pomifera), and some long and tapering (R. alpina); and big, sturdy Currant-bushes, laden with rich red bunches, the worth of which the peasantry appear to ignore, although they drive a brisk trade with the hotels in wild mountain Raspberries, Strawberries, and Bilberries. Is there, by the way, any known good reason why the fruit of the true Alpine Strawberry and the true Alpine Eglantine should be elongated rather than oval, as in the Strawberry and Eglantine of the plains? Circumstance must be at the root of the cause for this change, and it would be extremely interesting to be able to trace it. But this thought is only en passant.

Mention of the Bilberry warns us that we must not forget the dwarfer shrubs, lending as they do so much of warm, attractive colouring to the mountainside. First and foremost place must be given to the little Cowberry (Vaccinium vitis idoea), laden with its bright red and rose clusters, which the peasants manufacture into jam and wine; it is often in the company of Arbutus, or Arctostaphylos Uva Ursi, the Bearberry, with scarlet fruit of astringent medicinal qualities. Then there is Vaccinium uliginosum, with blue-black fruit, edible - though harmful in large quantities - and somewhat smaller than the Bilberry, by the side of which it is frequently found, and with which it is frequently confounded. The latter plant - the Bilberry (V. myrtillus) - is productive of an astringent jam used in cases of dysentery; also of an agreeable syrup and a fermented wine, besides providing an excellent dessert-fruit, whose stain is ruination to the table-linen!

Here, then, is an outline of what Autumn has to offer to those who court her in the Alps; surely not a season upon which to turn our backs in fear of ennui? It is a pity that the majority of visitors, obedient to Tradition, should so much shun the mountains at this time of year, and, as September arrives, make haste to gain the towns. By such unquestioning obedience are they robbed of much that is delightful, much also that is profitable. Facts prove that over and over again they worsen rather than better their circumstance. Facts prove that, generally speaking, Autumn is finer in the mountains than in the towns. Often and often a damp, grey fog will hold possession of the plains whilst the mountains are basking under a cloudless sky. Indeed, one of the grandest, most impressive of autumnal sights in the Alps is the vast billowy sea of fog which day by day will he choking the plains and valleys beneath. As we stand in the pure air and glorious sunshine, gazing across this ocean, and thinking of all those who, to escape from dismal and discomforting Autumn in the Alps, have fled down into this unwholesome state of things, we cannot suppress a smile - a broad, 'superior' smile - so manifest are the disadvantages of listening too closely to what

Tradition has to say. It is usual for Ignorance to congratulate itself upon its disabilities, and those in the towns, shivering in their furs, whilst regarding the grey skies above them, will be congratulating themselves upon having quitted the mountains betimes, and upon having at least the distractions of town-life to set against the chill and gloomy weather. Little do they reck, these good, customary souls, how that, really, the laughter and congratulation is ours, as we, under a canopy of spotless, radiant blue, gaze down upon the mirk into which, with so much good faith, they have been pleased to plunge themselves.

Hay-Fields At The Col De La Forclaz In July, With The Mountains Of The Valley Of Bagnes.

And if, after some days, or even weeks, of this unequal rule, the fog will commence to rise and envelop us in our turn - well, there is compensation enough for all who love Nature in a weird, mysterious mood. The mountains are the grander for the 'White mists which choke the vale, and blot the sides Of the bewildered hills.'

They tower up higher than ever they do on a clear, still day. All that we do not see of them adds enormously to the importance of the glimpses we catch here and there. As the turbulent veil of grey-white mist rives in places, giving us peeps of the snows and blue-green ice of some mighty glacier, or, maybe, of the warm red and orange of some Bilberry-covered slope, the effect is fairylike in the extreme, and we wish to see nor more nor less. Moreover, the scene is for ever changing. Endless are the combinations as the ceaselessly shifting mass of mist thins and evaporates here and thickens and reforms elsewhere. And when from out the mist comes the piercing, scream-like call of some sentinel Marmot on the far-off rocks; the shrill whistle of the Choughs now descending from the region of the glaciers; the twittering of migrating Swallows as they sweep upwards in hundreds from the plains; and the dull, fluctuating roar of some racing torrent in a gorge below - when such appropriate cries and sounds as these are added to the already fascinating scene, its eloquent suggestiveness is complete, and we have, indeed, a fitting 'curtain' to our Alpine year!

CHAPTER IX. ON THE ABUSE AND PROTECTION OF ALPINES

Hearing for the first time that there are gardens in the Alps, our irresistible impulse is to exclaim, 'Of course there are! the Alps are one vast and glorious garden!' And when at length we fully realize what is meant: that artificial gardens really do exist in the Alps - gardens, too, for Alpine plants - we feel the immediate appropriateness of crying, 'Coals to Newcastle!' Alpine gardens in the plains are understandable, explicable, delightful, filling a void and supplying a want; but Alpine gardens in the Alps themselves! - wherein is their rhyme and reason? Why should Man ape Nature when and where she is so ample, so supreme? Is it not idle, is it not even impertinent, for him to thrust his 'spurious imitations' into the very home and kingdom of what he presumes to imitate? Is it not what Thoreau would have called another egregious attempt on Man's part 'to plant his hoof among the stars'? Gardening, in some of its ways, may be an art which 'doth mend Nature,' but it is hard to believe that one of these ways is in meddling with the Alpine flora in its splendid, perfect home; even the 'universal mind' of Shakespeare could scarcely have had the Alps and their flowers in view when he spoke as he did of gardening!

But what at first sight seems such an anomaly is, in point of fact, a most pertinent and important undertaking. For although 'Les Alpes nous gardent encore Sur quelques sommets preserves, Des jardins que le monde ignore Et que Dieu seul a cultives' although Nature's own gardens abound in the Alps, this was not enough. Man, with his blind eye turned towards to-morrow, had for long been exercising his sweet, unfettered will, working sad havoc amongst the Alpine vegetation. Some means had to be devised to save him from himself, to correct or circumvent his wrong-headedness, to give some sight to his blind eye, and so to stave off as far as possible any further and final designs he might have upon the remnants of those varieties he had so nearly exterminated. Something had to be done, too, to try and counteract the designs which Nature herself seems to have upon the existence of certain species. A timely helping hand had, therefore, to be extended, and preserves had to be organized where menaced plants could find a refuge and live and multiply in comparative security.

Hence, the wisdom of Shakespeare is once more demonstrated, and gardening, even Alpine gardening, 'doth mend Nature.' Nor is human nature excluded from the mending. 'The garden is a potent maker of character,' and the influence of these particular gardens and of the societies governing them is already felt in the notable increase of intelligent appreciation and careful interest for the 'scented miracles' of the Alps. 'Coals to Newcastle' these gardens may be to some extent; but just as, by all accounts, there will come a time when Newcastle will be glad of coals from anywhere, so the Alps and lovers of Alpine circumstance, and even the world in general, will some day thank these gardens and the men whose foresight and perseverance have led to the creation of them at so right a moment.

Human labour is rewarded largely by additional labour. Man's activity obliges him to be incessantly and increasingly active. Since the dawn-days of his intelligence, when he commenced to cease accepting things as they were, and started to impose himself and his ideas upon Nature and prove himself in very deed her 'insurgent son' - since those dim and dawning days he has meddled and muddled to such an extent that, do what he now may, he is inextricably compromised. To make life possible, to enjoy a modicum of peace and to reap a modicum of beauty, he must, with less and less muddle, continue to meddle. Complications of his own contriving will beset him and undo him if he cease from strenuous meddling. Having put his hand to the plough, there can be no question of him loosing his hold or of turning back. On and on must he plough, furrow after furrow, in every direction, in every sort of ground, ever deeper, ever further afield, and with no limit yet in sight to all he has still to plough. Verily, 'The Eden of modern progress is a kitchen-garden!' - ay, more than that: a 'French' kitchen-garden - a garden of 'intensive culture'! A diagnosis of man's position shows that it is not unlike that of 'Poor Mrs. Somebody,' who 'swallowed a fly.' One thing leads to another; one remedy calls for a further remedy, usually upon a scale of rising importance, until contingencies which at one time would have appeared hair-brained and impossible are towering over him, live and threatening facts, rendering his condition positively and compulsorily heroic.

In short, and in a time-worn phrase, man has upset the balance of Nature. And all his efforts to restore this balance only bring him fresh problems to solve, and lead him deeper and deeper into the labyrinthine ways of cause and effect and the maze-like mysteries of the unity of all things. By, for instance, introducing rabbits where by rights there was no provision for rabbits, or by planting the Water - Hyacinthe in rivers not organized for its right reception, or by exterminating hawks and stoats where there was good and useful room for these, he brings about his ears undreamed of and unpleasant complications the fighting of which keeps him anxiously, nervously alert. Already, too, there are whispers of what untoward effect wireless telegraphy may have upon the weather; and it seems not unreasonable to wonder what changes may not be gradually wrought in the habits of birds and beasts when man comes to fly as easily as he walks.

Saxifrage, Saponaria, The Sulphur Anemone, And The Alpine Eglantine, With The Aiguille Du Tour And Glacier Des Grands. July.

But perhaps it is his improvidence which costs him the most dear. Incalculable trouble is saved by economy; but economy bespeaks a careful foresight, and it is rather among man's primary instincts to live largely for the moment, soothing himself with a muddle-headed reading of "Sufficient for the day———" All over the globe his haphazard destruction of the forests has involved him in painful experiences, the end of which still lies with the future. Nowhere, perhaps, is this more plainly felt and seen than in some parts of Switzerland, where the consequent erosion of the mountain-sides has brought about many a disastrous landslip, to say nothing of the deleterious effect upon the climate and the fertility of the soil. Possibly, the extermination of mountain flowers is a less serious matter - that is to say, from a material or practical and utilitarian point of view. Possibly, it may be a matter more of sentiment than of anything else.

It is well, however, to preface this opinion with the word 'possibly': for who, with the past as precedent, shall dare to say that the philosophy of even the wisest can so encompass this question as to foresee and weigh every remote and obscure contingency, and predict to the full the intricate effect which would accrue? The loss to Science, to mention only one consequence, would be immense. Plants, assuredly, in telling us about themselves, have much yet to tell us about ourselves and our planet, and the premature extinction of possibly important links in the chain of evidence would be an irredeemable mischief. Nature-study - that study which draws the sciences from their separate existences to a common centre, and induces them to act reciprocally in unravelling the secrets of the universe - Nature-study, comprehensive and systematic, is only in its youth, and the part which plants (particularly those highly specialized dwellers in the Alps) have to play in this study may be of greater moment than we at present can conceive. As with the Alpine vegetation of Rowenzori, in the Congo, so with the flora of the Swiss Alps: there is amongst it an essentially primitive element, an element that can give word of prehistoric circumstance, and possibly help to solve much that at present remains unexplained. The flora of Switzerland, as M. Henry Correvon points out, may be considered as the synthesis of that of Europe. Its diversity, especially in the Canton of Valais, is extraordinary. In this canton the flowers of every European climate are represented: flowers of the Mediterranean: flowers even of the Eastern steppes and deserts: flowers such as the brilliant Adonis vernalis, the equally brilliant Ranunculus gramineus, the yellow Wallflower, the large Periwinkle, the yellow Achillea, the blue Iris, the red Valerian, the rosy Bulbocodium, the purple Anemone, the blue Hyssop, the poisonous Lettuce, the curious Ephedra Helvetica, the rare Campanula excisa, the yellow Cactus (opuntia), and the feather-like Stipa pennata, with which the peasants, guides, and tourists so often decorate their hats. It is, then, for a flora such as this - a flora which, by reason of its unique nature, must yet prove of inestimable use to Science - that the Society for the Protection of Plants has taken up arms, and, amongst other activities, has fostered the formation of gardens.

But if mere sentiment were the only thing at stake, even on that score the destruction of the flora would probably have a most mischievous effect. The dearth of varied, cheerful loveliness in this direction could not but react unhealthily upon our character by injuring our outlook and thus impairing our capacity. To quote a passage from a Spanish source, used as a motto by the Swiss Association pour la Protection des Plantes upon the title-page of its yearly reports: 'If you wish to understand the importance of plants, imagine a world without them, and the comparison will alarm you, because the idea of death will at once present itself.' No doubt there are many people who will pooh-pooh this line of argument as high-flown and sickly - people who are ready to assert that life is too stern, too serious a business for that we should be expending our energies in defence of such immaterial and sentimental luxuries as are the flowers. The question, however, cannot be rightly dismissed in this superficial manner; it is far from being the frivolous one which these good people would have us believe. Subtleties are of the very life-blood of creation; and the subtle influence of the flowers upon the lives and characters of men, lying largely as it does beneath the surface and amongst the hidden vitalities of existence, escapes the off-hand, hasty glance or the so-called matter-of-fact view. Maybe we Europeans do not show this influence so strongly as do, for instance, the Japanese; maybe our thought, our art, our lives, are not so perceptibly affected; maybe that our philosophy has more of a personal character than has that of this Eastern people, and that we are more self-conscious and less abandoned children of Nature. Be all this as it may, Goddess Flora sits firmly and effectively enthroned within our lives, subtly ruling us to our very great and very real advantage. Ruskin was right, and ' Flowers seem intended for the solace of ordinary humanity.

Children love them; quiet, tender, contented, ordinary people love them as they grow; luxurious and disorderly people rejoice in them gathered. They are the cottager's treasure; and in the crowded town mark, as with a little broken fragment of rainbow, the windows of the workers in whose heart rests the covenant of peace.' Yes; Ruskin was right: in one way or another the flowers are loved by all; and the effect of this love, even though it be the love of 'luxurious and disorderly people,' filters down to most unexpected depths of our being, purifying our outlook upon life to an extent to which, for the most part, we are ignorant. And it is, above all, to this influential love - this healthy, important, ay, this even vital sentiment - for the flowers that the Swiss Society for the Protection of Plants commenced in 1883 to address itself in favour of the Alpine flora, seeking to augment and strengthen this sentiment in the popular breast by giving it a firmer basis in the popular intelligence.

Not without many preliminary failures have these gardens been established in the Alps. From one cause or another - from the unsuitability of the site selected, from the death of the founder, or from apathy on the part of the public in the matter of funds - garden after garden had to be abandoned and left to the tender mercies of goats and tourists - 'ces rasoirs du globe,' who, vulture-like, soon left little else but the dry bones. At length, however, with experience bought and enthusiasm aroused 'to sticking point,' several gardens have been firmly established, and are flourishing abundantly, not only as refuges for floral rarities, but also as distilleries of a purer-principled public spirit with regard to the flora in general. And each year sees fresh gardens springing up, educating the popular mind. For it is not alone against the depredations of the tourist that this movement is directed. It is aimed quite as much, and even more directly, at the herbalist, at the collector for nurseryman and florist, and at the peasant who hawks the rarer plants on the markets of the villages and towns. The rapacious collector who sends plants out of their native country by thousands is by no means peculiar to the Swiss Alps; he is prowling about all over the globe, openly vaunting his 'cuteness' in removing every vestige of this or that plant from its native habitat. Something had to be done to correct this man's morals, or make him ashamed or afraid to put them into practice, at any rate in Switzerland. What North Borneo could do for its Orchids surely Switzerland could do for its Alpines. Culling an apt phrase from 'Major Barbara': 'Morality that doesn't fit the facts - "scrap" it !'; and this the Society for the Protection of Plants set itself to accomplish, with the result that to-day the rapacious vandal is virtually stamped out.

The Society and its offshoots, the gardens, have also dealt most effectively with the unthinking habits of the peasant, who sought to enrich himself by selling rudely uprooted rarities on the markets or among the hotels - by, in fact, killing the goose which laid the golden eggs. He has been brought to see that it is better all-round policy to cultivate the plants from seeds; and this he has begun to do in, for example, the district around the Saleve, near Geneva. His customers, also, have learnt some wisdom, now recognizing more or less that plants so raised are far better worth buying than the poor, withered, mutilated specimens carelessly uprooted from the mountains. Indeed, under the old conditions, these customers foolishly paid four or five times the catalogue price of sound, acclimatized roots and bulbs for maimed and half-dead plants roughly snatched, often forty-eight hours or more previously, from their wild home. Then, again, local authorities in many parts of the country have been induced to take steps for the strict preservation of whatever flowers are menaced with extinction. In this way Cyclamen europoeum, for instance, is receiving special and timely protection in Savoy; Gentiana lutea in the Swiss Tyrol; Iris virescens around Sion; Cypripedium Calceolus in the Rhone Valley and other districts; Androsace Vitelliana at Zermatt; Campanula excisa at Saas-Fee; Androsace Charpentieri in the Canton of Ticino; Pyrola umbellata in the Commune of Andelfingen, Canton of Zurich; Cerinthe alpina in the Jura; Adonis vernalis in the Rhone Valley; Tulipa silvestris at Bex and around Geneva; Erythronium Dens-canis around Geneva; and Eryngium alpinum and Atra-gene alpina wherever they are to be found.

The movement, then, is not of mushroom growth. It has meant many years of ceaseless endeavour, often anxious, often dispiriting, and often prosecuted with an imperative degree of patient diplomacy. Unaided at first by the Government, it lacked authority to impose its principles. Its appeal was to the public conscience; and this latter is notoriously apt to be a little hard of hearing. But M. Henry Correvon (President of the Society until, in 1908, it was absorbed by the Heimathschutz or Ligue Suisse pour la Protection des Beautes Naturelles), with untiring effort and unquenchable enthusiasm, has gained its ear and aroused its proper pride. To this gentleman, indeed, all lovers of the Alpine flora owe an inestimable debt, one which must only increase as time rolls on. He has devoted himself heart and soul to attain his object. Visiting England, Belgium, France, and Italy in order to win over nurserymen, importers, and the gardening world in general to the idea that it is better to raise from seed than to root up, he has lectured to this end in these countries. He has lectured, also, in the mountain towns and villages of Switzerland and Savoy to the local authorities, guides, and peasantry, trying to instil respect for the lovely denizens of their Alps. Director of the successful gardens on the Rochers de Naye and at Bourg St. Pierre, he has a wonderfully efficient garden of his own at Geneva ('Floraire,' originally the Geneva Acclimatization Gardens, but acquired by M. Correvon in 1893), the main object of which is to furnish plants, but especially seeds, to botanical gardens, and to gardeners and plant-lovers generally.

M. Correvon once insisted (it was in 1896, at the General Meeting of the Society) that the aim of the Society was not to prevent lovers of flowers from bringing back from their Alpine excursions living souvenirs for the adornment of their rockeries, but to arrest the professional collector's wholesale depredations; and, of course, this must be accepted as exact. Nevertheless, the more modest pilferings of the excursionist and tourist have been affected by the movement quite as markedly, by comparison, as have the wholesale plunderings of the professional collector. The cause of the persecuted Alpines has been won; and it has been won not merely amongst a particular section of the public, but also amongst the mountain peasantry. A popular spirit of patriotic pride in the country's flora has been aroused, and, so to speak, polices the mountains; consequently, every class of collector is affected. Nor, really, is this the least happy of the Society's achievements. For the total amount of destruction wrought by the whole vast army of tourists and excursionists must have been great, although each individual sum may have been small. And most often it was idle destruction - purely and simply idle and unthinking. Lovers have still much to learn of how to be loving; and the lover of plants can be as enthusiastically inconsiderate as any other lover. Flower-loving tourists are more frequently to be dreaded than they who are 'dead to love' in this regard. More often than not the flowers are far better cared for by the tourist who is utterly indifferent to their charms: for he leaves them alone! Oh that all flowers had the traditional gift of Atropa Mandragora (the Mandrake) - to shriek out aloud when pulled up by the roots! The cry might affect to good purpose the 'disorderly' flower-lover! Seemingly, like the proverbial boy who must fling a murderous stone at any beautiful bird, the tourist, as soon as he sees a lovely flower - some particularly well-grown specimen or some rare white form - is apt to feel that it must be uprooted and taken home. The same idle impulse - the impulse to possess, and the impulse to kill in order to possess - seizes boy and tourist alike, and usually with a like result: the bird is soon thrown aside to moulder, whilst the plant is left to rot in water or to lie waterless in the sun on the window-sill of some hotel bedroom. The reckless and destructive element in this impulse to possess 'root and branch' was strikingly illustrated in the early summer of 1908. During a ten-days absence of the gardener, a number of lovely Alpines were uprooted from the garden on the summit of the Rochers de Naye, above Montreux, many of the plants being left lying scattered here and there, spurned, probably, as redundant by the impulsive lover!

Arnica And Campanula Barbata On The Col De La Forclaz, At The End Of July.

In certain ways the tourist uprooter is the more difficult and delicate element to deal with in the whole problem; but the Society has, by the 'sweet reasonableness' of its moral persuasion, arrived at a very fair and effective solution. Much as comes a guest comes the tourist to the Alps, and his coming is one of the main sources of the country's prosperity. His peccadilloes are for the most part overlooked, and he enjoys a freedom such as is scarcely his at home. This, generally speaking, is, of course, the case with non-residents or visitors anywhere; but in Switzerland it is, perhaps, particularly marked. Not infrequently, however, his special privileges are lost upon the tourist, and he forthwith helps himself to still more freedom. He must not be surprised, then, if he is met with framed and reasonable restrictions; he must not be vexed if, in his hotel or pension, he finds an Avis aux Touristes exhorting him in formal terms to allow the flora to bide where it is. He should not feel this to be an attack upon his liberty.

Ah, ' there's the rub !' - there, in that little word 'liberty,' lies largely the root of the matter. Alike for Swiss and for foreigner; alike for collector, peasant, and tourist, this word holds the key to the greater part of the necessity for the protection of Alpine plants. It is the old, old story: men mouth the word, but miss its finest flavour. Irresistibly one is reminded of certain of Juste Olivier's well-known lines:

'Vraiment, quel sujet de satire! Alors qu'on voit tout un peuple en delire Qui se dit libre. . . .'

It is the old, old story: the story that has caused jungle, 'park,' and forest to be set aside for the fauna of India, America, and Africa; that has necessitated a close time for birds; that has required a protective cordon to be drawn around the Matter-horn; and that has made it imperative to create 'jardins-refuges' for the flowers of the Alps - the old, old story of licence being supposed to spell liberty. If certain of the public think that liberty is menaced by the Ligue Suisse, it is from a faulty comprehension of the word's best meaning. The Society makes no attack upon liberty. Why, 'Liberty's in every blow!' Every blow dealt by the movement is dealt on the side of healthy enjoyment and delight; every blow, therefore, is dealt on the side of one of the prime elements in true liberty. If the Society deals blows at anything, it is at licence. It battles for law and order, and its battles are on the side of the angels - on the side of the veriest of platitudes: 'Without law and order, there is no true liberty.' To allow the individualist's reading of the word would be to allow freedom to clash with liberty; egotistical individualism in freedom is only too apt to be one of Liberty's direst enemies. Mr. Dooley, with his usual quaint acumen, says: 'A man can't be indipindint onless he has a boss'; and in this present case the necessary boss is the Ligue. Without it we should continue to have such freedom as would extinguish the Edelweiss around Zermatt as it has extinguished the Chamois around Chamounix.

Men for ages have been singing hymns to Liberty in the Alps of Switzerland, but never before, probably, have they sung to finer effect than since the Society for the Protection of Plants took the field and spread additional light. Liberty has received a larger, wider meaning, and never has hymn been sung with truer significance than to-day is Eugene Rambert's inspiring song, 'Les Alpes':

> 'Voici la cime altiere,
> Au front audacieux, D'ou l'aigle temeraire
> Va visiter les cieux. O celestes campagnes!
> Nature! immensite! Chantons sur nos montagnes,
> Chantons la liberte!1

CHAPTER X. IN AN ALPINE GARDEN

A visit to an Alpine garden is like a visit to an Orchid-house: it is a unique experience. Our sensations are quite other than when visiting a Herbaceous border. For of all plants, Alpines and Orchids surround themselves with an atmosphere all their own. On visiting one or other of the well-established gardens in the Alps, we are instantly impressed with a feeling that here is no ordinary garden. It is as though we entered the Sanctum-of-Sanctums of plant-life. Ignorant as we may be of the plants themselves, of their history, of their capacities and aptitudes, we fall under the sway of some subtle spell, and are affected as we are never affected in a Rose-garden. And this is because, knowingly or unknowingly, we are in the presence of the very highest asceticism. Whether we realize it or not, here is a great and varied concourse of ascetics gathered from the four corners of the Alpine world - ascetics in the truest, noblest sense happy, laughing, vigour-full, enjoying life as only true ascetics can. Whether we realize it or not, here is a gathering of plants which have become supremely lovely under the severest conditions - plants which have renounced the 'pomps and vanities,' the superabundance and grossness of the world, and so have attained to a refinement and brilliance of beauty which even tropical vegetation, at the other end of the scale, must envy. Whether we realize all this or not, the effect upon us is much the same: in an Alpine garden we feel that we should doff our hats and speak in whispers, for we are conscious of being in the presence of 'A deeper radiance than mere light can give.'

Speaking of Alpines, the author of 'Studies in Gardening' says that, 'of all plants they have the most character'; and it is, indeed, possible that they are the last and highest word upon character in the Vegetable Kingdom. Alpines tend, as it were, to complete the circle of vegetable circumstance. Commencing with lichens on the rocks, vegetation progresses, as soil accumulates and becomes richer and deeper, order above order, along a scale of increasing organism, until trees appear and the soil has reached its highest degree of development.

Alpine Garden (La Linnea) At Bourg St. Pierre, On The Road To The Grand St. Bernard. At The Beginning Of August.

Vegetation, however, does not stop here on the scale; it continues to ascend, and, in doing so, is satisfied with less and less soil. As the line of progress arches over, Alpines appear. With them, especially with the higher Alpines, there is a minimum of soil and a maximum of organization. With them the circle of vegetable circumstance is approximately complete. For whereas the lichens, because of their primitive organism, are able to live on the rocks, the Alpines are doing much the same because of their high and complex organism.

The temptation is to extend the thought, and to attempt a parallel between this cycle of circumstance and our own: for there is a strong suggestion here of the presence of one simple, vast, and sympathetic purpose underlying all creation - a suggestion that humanity is not exempt from that same purpose which directs the plants. There is, too, a suggestion of help '. . .to those agrope In the mad maze of hope, a suggestion of the delicate truth expressed by Richard Jefferies, that 'every blade of grass, each leaf, each separate floret and petal, is an inscription speaking of Hope.' Shall we attempt the parallel? Shall we say that man began his course in the simplicity of Eden, content and capable in that simplicity because he himself was simple; that he was as a lichen on a rock? That since then the trend of his course has been, and is, towards a return to Eden, where he will live and thrive because of his new simplicity begot of thorough complexity; that he will have become as an Alpine on a rock? For whereas he was ignorantly simple, he is becoming wisely simple. Through all luxuriance, superabundance, and grossness, he is wending his way: to end content and capable amid the severity of Alpine conditions. Not clothless, grubbing for nuts and lentils, as the complex 'Simple Life' of to-day would so much have him; but a gorgeously simple prince in a palace, rid of all exaggeration and make-believe, devoid of all untimeliness, entirely unsophisticated, utterly natural - Nature's wisest, richest, most splendid ascetic.

But there is something more than metaphysical and other abstractions to be garnered from a visit to an Alpine garden in the Alps! There is much of great practical worth to those who possess a rockery at home, or who purpose building one. For whatever a rock-garden may be elsewhere, here in the Alps it is more than Mr. Eden Phillpotts suggests: it is more than 'merely a theatre for the display of hundreds of little plants.' Here, in an hour or so, the visitor can gather an amount of information and experience equal, and possibly superior, to any he may amass in weeks of touring over the mountains. The seeking out of Alpines in their wild state has, of course, its indisputable value; but - and this is by no means rare - much may be noticed during these rambles which is liable to mislead if experience of the Alps and their flora is but slight. The tourist-observer is apt to meet with plants in exceptional circumstance, and to take note of this circumstance as if it were the rule. If, then, on his return home, he there treats such plants according to the experience he gathered of them in the Alps, he is more than likely to find that he has been led astray.

Let us take a case in point. Let us take, for instance, Gentiana verna, one of the most widely distributed of Alpines in Switzerland, and yet, by all accounts, one with which but small success is achieved in England. Now, the visitor will, if he follow a very general custom, only arrive in the Alps when this Gentian has gone out of flower on the pastures, its usual home. If he find it in flower at all, it will probably be higher up and upon rocks with a north aspect. (We are not speaking of any-disputed or reputed form of Gentiana verna, such as G. brachyphylla, but of the true type-plant.) I have myself so found it in July, perched up on the precipices of the Rochers de Naye, some 6,800 feet. But this cannot be considered characteristic of the plant; it is here in an exceptional, rather than habitual, position. It is not what is usually called a rock-plant. However, the observer, not having seen it in all its normal abundance on the pastures earlier in the year, is liable to take note of its isolated position on the rocks, and to treat it accordingly when he gets home. Success can scarcely attend his efforts.

Careless as we generally are, it now and again happens that we try to outdo Nature in carefulness. When we sow flower-seed, we choose a likely spot and watch it (blaming our seedsman if the seed should fail to germinate). But Nature takes no such pains; she has a larger way of being careful. Paradoxical as ever, she proceeds with amazing yet studious prodigality. To make quite sure of catching a sprat, she, so to speak, baits her hook with a whale; she strews the seed broadcast to the four winds everywhere, and it may come up where it can. It is for this reason that we meet with such erratic instance as that of Spiraea ulmaria growing along a damp, rocky cleft high up above the Grand St. Bernard road, a little beyond the village of Liddes - and growing, too, to all appearances, as happily as it grows among the marshes by the Rhone. We could never hope to grow it on a rock like this in our gardens. Plants in the wild state, with freedom of choice, can often grapple with seemingly adverse conditions by ways and means so subtle that they defy imitation in a garden. Moreover, if we knew all, when we find them, like this Spiraea or like Gentiana verna, flourishing though exceptionally placed, we should be aware that their circumstance was importantly allied to normal circumstance, and that they have found in this position the vital essentials of their ordinary life. But in a garden we must not think to treat a species after the successful eccentricity we have noted in some individual of that species; and it is in this, among other important matters, that the gardens in the Alps can offer so much useful direction. Here we are afforded a ready means of studying hundreds of different plants tended by experts, and growing, as far as is possible, according to the normal requirements of each individual kind.

And yet the visitor must remember that these gardens are in every sense Alpine. That is to say, he must remember that they are more or less subject to Alpine conditions - to, for instance, the long snows of winter and all that those snows mean. Therefore, much of what is learnt from these gardens must afterwards be made to fit in with the conditions of the home garden - with, for instance, the humidity of winter or the comparative dryness of spring. Let us again take the case of Gentiana verna as illustration. It loves moisture rather than dryness, especially during its flowering season. This moisture it obtains, in Switzerland, from the gradually melting snow; but on a rock-work in England it is not likely to have this steady supply of moisture. If placed upon a slope in the rockery, in imitation of its position on a sloping Alpine pasture, though it may receive the Spring rains, these will rapidly run off, leaving the slope dry again almost immediately. Although it abhors any approach to stagnant moisture, this Gentian cannot be treated like a rock-loving Saxifrage or Sedum, nor, be it remembered, like a deep-growing, tap-rooted Campanula or Phyteuma. For it to meet with anything like enjoyment, it should be planted in a well-drained, loamy hollow or depression in the rockwork, where, although exposed to all possible sunshine, it may benefit most by the rains.

The science of putting two and two together in order to make four is nowhere more essential than in the culture of Alpines away from their wild conditions. If thoughtful common-sense is a sine qua non of successful gardening, it is certainly never more so than of rock-gardening. Hardy as Alpines would appear, and as, indeed, they are usually styled, they often prove to be delicate subjects when removed from the severe yet logical conditions of their home-life; and those of them which flourish under the poorest, severest conditions in the Alps are those which, generally speaking, are the most difficult to deal with in captivity. To succeed in keeping a plant alive is not always the same thing as growing it successfully. Some plants may know how to adapt themselves more or less to unusual conditions, but this adaptation is not evolution; it is of a kind which lays siege to, and saps, vitality, and the life and character of such plants must suffer. In this domain a visit to a garden in the Alps can be of the very greatest assistance.

The Yellow Gentian At The End Of August, With The Col De Balme And Mont Blanc In The Distance.

In these gardens, also, it may be seen that rock-gardening does not consist in simply putting a plant upon a rock or amongst a pile of stones, but that it begins with the very foundations of the rockwork. It may be seen how the natural character of the site has been adapted; how the artificial rockeries have been constructed; how carefully every aspect has been built up; how thoughtfully every crack and crevice has been used; how every slope, every hollow, every pocket, has a meaning; and, above all, how perfectly the drainage has been maintained throughout. For the purpose of noting these things, an early visit (say towards the beginning of June) is often of great advantage. At that season the gardeners may be caught busily reconstructing the older portions of the rockeries and ridding them of deep-seated weeds: for all is not select even in Alpine refinement. Such occasions will afford striking instance of the methodical work which rockwork-building is - when understood. To be noted, too, is the class of rock or rocks it is desirable to employ. No clinkers, flints, tiles, glazed bricks, broken china, or large sea-shells will here be found: for these 'beautifying' constituents of many an English rockwork are taboo. Here is purely a 'business concern.' Nor, for that reason, does it lack in beauty. Quite the reverse: it is too realistic to be ugly. Statues, fountains, goldfish and such-like accessories could add not one jot or tittle to its fascination. Many a rock-garden in England is reminiscent of the story of a Japanese gentleman who, taken to see an elaborate and costly 'Japanese' garden in the counties, declared with delightfully ambiguous enthusiasm- 'It is wonderful! Marvellous! We have nothing like it!'

There is also admirable occasion for the botanist in these gardens: an enlarging opportunity which his Herbarium can scarcely supply. If Botany is, as the dictionary says it is, 'the natural history of plants,' then it is not merely a question of microscope and Latin names; it is the all-round study and knowledge of plants. What is often spoken of as Botany tends too much to 'drive out nature with a fork,' and our conversation with distinguished botanists is too often a talk with what Emerson would call 'accomplished persons who appear to be strangers in nature.' There are, indeed, some botanists who take no interest whatever in the live plant, and who look upon those who do as 'gardeners.' In the 'Memorials' of Professor C. C. Babington is told a story of how a Newnham girl saw a saucer-full of the red fungus Peziza coccinea and exclaimed, 'Oh! how beautiful! What is it V and when told it was Peziza, she said she had 'been working at that for a week'! Mathematical observation as a department in Botany is, of course, of inestimable value; but it can hardly lay claim to make a complete and final statement of the whole matter. Readily may we grant that 'They only know what Nature means Who watch the play behind the scenes'; but the 'gardener' gets behind the scenes quite as efficiently as does the 'botanist,' and he sees things of which the 'botanist' frequently never dreams. But what may be called the School of Realistic Botany is rapidly gaining ground. We are coming to see that we can be a little too jealously inclined to condemn our sciences to separate and solitary confinement. We are coming to see that no speciality can stand alone in any final sense and yet speak the full, round truth; and that, vital as is particularization, generalization is no less important, and must, in the end, be allowed 'the last word.'

Then, again, a visit to a garden in the Alps offers a convenient opportunity for examining some of the numerous theories concerning Alpines. For example, one of these theories is that the proportion of white and yellow flowers to those which are red, blue, and mauve, is less in the Alps than in the plains. It is a theory which has been put forward both by Dr. Percy Groom and Mr. H. Stuart Thompson, and it is one which is perhaps debatable. Mr. Thompson holds that blues, reds, and purples, are not only more abundant in quantity in the Alps than in the plains, but also, though possibly to a less extent, in species; and he cites the Gentians and Campanulas as example. Now I do think that the gardens can throw some light upon this matter, at any rate with regard to the question of species; with regard to quantity, of course, we must appeal to the wild slopes, rocks, and pastures. My own experience is that, at all events in spring, these Alpine rock-gardens show a striking abundance of white, cream, and yellow flowers, whereas there is but a goodly number of red and mauve flowers, and comparatively few that are blue. That is in the Spring. Later, it is true, the blue flowers increase considerably: and yet, white and cream and yellow blossoms seem to continue to hold their own. Mr. Thompson instances the large tribe of Campanulas and Gentians as an argument for the existence of a preponderance of blue. But against these may be set almost the whole army of Saxifrages and Ranunculus; for, with but few red or mauve exceptions, the Saxifrages are white, cream, and yellow, and, with the exception of Ranunculus glacialis (which, after all, starts its career pure white and only turns red when the insects or the winds have inoculated it), the whole group of Ranunculus is either white or yellow. Moreover - and this is a common occurrence among blue flowers - almost every variety of blue Gentian has its white form, as also have very many of the blue Campanulas. I am inclined to think, therefore, that the balance of colour as regards species is very fairly maintained. Naturally, the only way to set the matter at rest would be to have a list of all the flowers of the Alps tabulated according to colour; but, speaking without such a list, I am inclined to think that if the theory has any foundation in fact, it is but slight - too slight for that it should be phenomenally striking.

Mr. Thompson has, possibly, better material with which to make a case for quantity. There is such an extraordinary wealth of red Rhododendron, blue Gentian, and purple Viola, in the Alps, that all other colours seem to be in a charming minority. But this is only in Spring or early Summer, and in certain landscapes. There are other landscapes at the same season which are yellow with the Globe Flower, or the Sulphur Anemone, each of which is accompanied by Buttercups and Dandelions, Rock Rose, Potentillas and Geums; while yet other landscapes are white with the Narcissus, the limestone-loving Windflower, or the Fair Maid of France (Ranunculus aconitifolius), associated with hosts of Marguerites, Bladder-Campions, and other white blossoms. Here again, then, there appears to be room for doubt: for it seems very much a question of district and of moment.

It is, perhaps, a pity to try and pull so pretty a theory to pieces, and I rather hope that my objections may be ill-founded. For the theory is one which admirably accords with the high nature of Alpine plants, particularly those with blue flowers. Whereas yellow flowers have generally the more primitive organism, blue flowers have the highest; and, to quote Dr. Percy Groom, 'In Alpine flowers there is a larger percentage of the colours corresponding genetically to high organization than there is in the lowland.' Now, the Mystic will tell you that blue is heaven's own colour; and surely it is not a little fascinating to think that the further heavenwards some plants climb, the more intense and profuse becomes the blue of their flowers (in the same way as it is fascinating to be able to think that the sweetness of flowers increases with the altitude, and that hives give a heavier yield of honey in the Alps than in the plains). Few will dispute what appears so obvious - that the blue of the Myosotis and the Gentian, and of Eritrichium nanum, 'King of the Alps,' the highest and brightest of all blue Alpines, is unmatched by any blue in the plains. And then, if red is also so predominant in these high altitudes - well, even here the mystic may have his word. He may say that red stands for the vigour of life, and that for due and proper worldli-ness it is possible to have too much blue; and he may quote as instance the unhealthy state which a thus-far perceptive world knows as 'a fit of the blues.' He may argue that, because of this, and because of the abundant blueness of Alpine circumstance, it is only proper that an abundance of red should exist to keep the healthy balance.

And more, in like strain, the Mystic might argue - if he were allowed! But he must not labour the subject here. We shall content ourselves in hoping with him that Dr. Groom and Mr. Thompson may be right in their theory. We shall hope this for the sake of the yet higher reputation and significance of Amine plants: those marvels which already contribute so much to 'expand the fifth sense of wonder.'

Thistles, Anthyllis, And The Apollo Butterfly, With The Aiguille Du Tour. September.

CHAPTER XI. SOME GARDENS IN THE ALPS

Gardens are becoming more and more numerous in the Alps; almost every year lengthens the list. For present purposes, however, we will content ourselves with visiting three only - three of the oldest and most representative; and, as Alpine plants may be roughly divided into two sections - the limestone-loving and the granite-loving - we shall be careful to choose a garden in a limestone, and one in a granite district; the third being one which is purely scientific, as apart from the more decorative and protectionist aim of the other two. We will also visit them in the order in which the writer last saw them in the Spring and Summer of 1909.

THE THOMASIA (LIMESTONE; ALTITUDE ABOUT 3,800 FT.)

An easy walk of some three and a half hours from Bex, in the Rhone Valley, this garden is admirably situated at Pont de Nant amid sheltered, park-like pastures above Les Plans and at the foot of the giant cliffs of the Grand Muveran. To the west lies the Dent de Morcles and Glacier de Martinet; to the east, Les Diablerets and the Col des Essets; while to the north is the lovely wooded gorge of the Avancon and the distant mountains of Savoy. Subsidized by the Canton de Vaud, and affiliated to the University of Lausanne, this garden is strictly scientific. But it is none the less beautiful for that, and in the middle of May it was redolent of joyous colour. Brilliant canary-yellow patches of the grey-green, moss-like Aretia Vitaliana; deep pink groups of Primula rosea; graceful little creamy-white bushes of Daphne Blagayana from Bosnia; intense blue-purple tufts of Viola Calcarata; compact, pure white masses of Saxifraga Salomonii and Saxifraga Petraschii; and bright chrome patches of Erysimum. Kotschyanum were aglow among the rocks in the hot midday sunshine. Regiments, too, of Primula Cashmeriana from India were rearing their erect, round heads above the lovely magenta flowers of Primula calycina from Lombardy, and the clear yellow clumps of Draba Olympica diversifolia from Armenia, and Draba bruniaefolia from Persia; whilst many another Primula and Saxifrage was adding its pure and lively colouring to a scene which was gay indeed, backed and enhanced as it was by the blue-grey haze enveloping the distant forests and glacier. In spite of the garden's scientific arrangement, its appeal to the mere lover of beauty is irresistible. How, indeed, could it be otherwise? - how could such lovely subjects be planted amid such lovely surroundings without the result being lovely? At this season of the year, moreover, everything noticeable among the plants is so diminutive, so refined, so typical of Alpine circumstance; resplendent asceticism: * sanctity which shames our religions, and reality which discredits our heroes!'

THE RAMBERTIA (LIMESTONE; ALTITUDE ABOUT 6,900 FT.)

Here, at the summit of the Rochers de Naye, above Montreux, is a garden which is one of the highest and most romantically situated in Europe. Laid out, for the most part, upon the southern face of a precipitous cliff, it is in striking contrast with the Pont de Nant garden. On a calm and cloudless day it is entirely fascinating, and, with the magnificent panorama of Alp-land stretching away on all sides, it is the very setting of which we dream for Alpine plants. But when the fierce northern or north-westerly gales are blowing from over the Jura, with, possibly, a driving, blinding snow or hail, it is not a particularly inviting spot to visit. Under such conditions, only the Chough seems happy, as, with a cheerful whistle, it hovers on the brink of the precipice, and rises and falls in the teeth of the tempest like some black Japanese bird-kite. But even then we may be instructed; for we obtain a glimpse of the kind of weather-fury which has so much to do with the making of Alpines.

Here, like the mice against which the gardener wages grim warfare, the Iceland Poppy appears to have found an ideal home. Eagerly it is invading the rocky escarpments on every hand, and nothing could be more charming than to see its pure orange, yellow, or white blossoms consorting with those of Anemone alpina, and nodding in the sunshine against a background of distant Jungfrau, Eiger, and Monch. Indeed, this Poppy is so thoroughly happy on the Rochers de Naye that quantities of it may be seen springing up even amongst the weather-worn asphalt on the terraces and balconies of the hotel. Primulas, too, were making a brave show in the garden - as bright and brave a show at the end of June as in the garden at the Pont de Nant they were making in the middle of May. Just inside the entrance-gate is a rock-work profusely studded with such rosy-magenta gems as Primulas latifolia, integrifolia, longiflora, venusta, calycina, hirsuta, marginata, minima, and Cash-meriana. Further on, along the path which winds down the face of the cliff, was a lovely white form of Viola calcarata, nestling with Saxifraga atro-purpurea, the rosy Androsace sempervivoides, and the 'Floraire' variety of Androsace Chumbyi Here, too, was the violet-veined Geranium argenteum, the yellow, marguerite-like Aronicum scorpioides, the exquisite and uncommon white form of Linaria alpina, the Caucasian Doronicum (with not so fine a flower as that of its Swiss relation), and a large and wonderfully rich blue form of Gentiana acaulis. In fact, in this garden, situated as it is, and not being strictly scientific, M. Henry Correvon has had more scope for attractive display than has Professor Wilczeck at the Pont de Nant. And the result is extremely fascinating. When no mists and clouds are drifting up from the Lake of Geneva, and we are wandering up and down the steep paths, peering into the many rugged nooks and corners decked with the floral treasures of the world's Alps, we cannot but imagine it a likely playground for mountain sprites and fairies.

THE LINNEA (GRANITE; ALTITUDE ABOUT 5,300 FT.)

Just outside, and dominating the quaint little village of Bourg St. Pierre - the last village upon the road to the Grand St. Bernard - stands the oldest of the gardens in the Swiss Alps: La Linnea. Founded in 1889 with M. Henry Correvon as director, it now affords shelter to some 3,000 different kinds of plants, of which some 2,000 appear to be perfectly happy and flourishing. Once again the Iceland Poppy has found for itself a congenial home - a home which it shares with the little Papaver alpina, of finer foliage and frailer blossom. But the garden has really no need to borrow the brilliance of these two Poppies - at all events, not at the end of July and beginning of August: for at that season its wealth is superabundant. Even along the shady paths which wind up about its northern side there is no lack of colour-interest; even here, in the shade, plants indigenous to the site, such as the rich madder-red Lilium Martagon, the warm-brown Gentian (G. purpurea) and its creamy relative, G. punctata, the rosy Adenostyles and the stately mauve Mulgedium, are mingling in more or less tended profusion with such strangers as the steel-blue Eryngium, the gleaming white Pyramidal Saxifrage, the rosy Rhododendron hirsutum and its American cousin, R. punctatum, of larger, clearer pink flowers. And when, after a time, the plateau at the summit of the garden is reached, we are met by an expanse of such varied, glowing colour as is indeed difficult to describe with any true degree of sufficiency. Although the plants are mainly grouped according to their countries, they are arranged with a keen eye to effect. The vivid orange Lilium croceum from the Simplon and the rich plum - coloured Verbascum phoeniceum are near neighbours of the lively-violet Campanula nobilis from Japan, of the brilliant orange Senecio Tyrolensis and of the fiery-sprayed Heuchera sanguinea from the Sierras of Mexico. Many kinds of lovely Columbines and Delphiniums are rubbing shoulders with the tall and decorative pale-yellow Scabious (Cephalaria), with the nobly-plumed Spiraea Aruncus, and with the deep brick-red Potentilla atrosanguinea from the Himalaya and the dwarf white Potentilla Clusiana from the Alps of Austria. Hosts of lovely Saxifrages and Androsaces, too, in infinite variety, are in neighbourly communion with a remarkably rich and varied collection of lovely Pinks. With these and many another bright and exquisite flower in abundance, what need for Papaver nudicaule, the Iceland Poppy, to lend its brilliance to the feast!

There are many things of beauty in this world about which we feel most eloquent when we remain dumb - things of beauty which we can sensibly appreciate more than we can explain; and it is among these things that we must place the mountain-flowers. Their fascination is so elusive a quantity that it quite defies adequate presentation by either pen or brush. What presentation we can make is of necessity in the manner of a mere 'prentice hand. Whether it be in the gardens or upon the wild mountain-side, the moment we set pen or brush to paper this elusiveness confronts us, and we are aware that we have sensed more than we can tell. Perhaps this is especially the case when we are gazing upon Alpines in all the attractiveness of freedom. Then, especially, is there a je-ne-sais-quoi of enchantment which sets us childishly fumbling upon our palette or among our parts of speech. We are filled with confused expression; adjectives are of small avail, and our brightest, deftest colour-blends are flat and lifeless.

How is it, by the way, that more attempts are not made in England to create Alpine pastures? Alpine rock-works we have in hundreds, but a stretch of meadow-land sown or planted with Alpine field-flowers seems as yet to be but rarely attempted. And yet, commencing with the bulbs and ending with the hay-flowers, what could be more interesting or seductive? Innumerable variety crammed into one small spot is not the secret of Nature's wild, unfettered loveliness.

A little way up the Valsorey, not far from the Sempervivum-decked roofs of Bourg St. Pierre, are some gentle, grassy slopes and long, low ridges of crumbling rock whose floral robe in July and August baffles description far more completely than anything to be seen in the gorgeous garden near by. Pinks, Campanulas, Phyteumas, Asters, Saxifrages, Arenarias and Veronicas are there growing in bewildering abundance, and yet with a grace and airy-lightness which is far more moving and far more difficult to translate than are the compact and studied masses in the garden. Though the beauty of this latter may well exhaust our fund of superlatives, these untamed slopes outside make an even higher, more elusive appeal. It is well to wander from the garden to these rocks and pastures, and mark how that 'the earned loaf eats the sweetest.' It is well to see how, in spite of all that Man may do to imitate and even to create, he cannot equal, much less rival, Nature. It is well to note, by contrast, the worth and quality of his 'creations': to see how his originality obliges him to imitate, and how wondrously original ofttimes are his imitations! It is well to note all this - to see how Nature obtains her gracious and triumphant effects, and how the exigencies of a garden (as we at present mostly understand a garden) oblige our best and loveliest endeavours to take but a back and distant seat. To those who have not seen these things side by side amid the grand and glorious setting of the Alps no wish of ours could be more friendly than that they may have speedy occasion to 'look in the sky to find the moon, not in the pool.'

OTHER ALPINE BOOKS

Uniform With This Volume Each Containing Full-Page Illustrations In Colour - The Alps By A. D. M'cormick And Sir Martin Conway Containing 62 Full-Page Illustrations Reproduced In The Colours Of The Originals 'A very delightful, and we would add, to the lover of great hills, a very soothing book.' - Spectator.

The Lake Of Geneva By J. Hardwicke Lewis, May Hardwicke Lewis, and Francis H. Gribble ontaining 60 Full-Page Illustrations Reproduced In The Colours Of The Originals Or can be had in three separate parts, viz.:

Geneva Containing 20 Full-Page Illustrations Reproduced In Colour 'This is a thoroughly enjoyable book, which ought to be read by everyone visiting Geneva.' - A berdeen Journal.

Lausanne - Containing 20 Full-Page Illustrations Reproduced In Colour 'This handsome volume.' - Man. hester Courier.

Montreux - Containing 20 Full-Page Illustrations Reproduced In Colour 'Skilful landscape paintings, very varied in subject, the letterpress ... is never dull.' - Times.

Our Life In The Swiss Highlands By J. Hardwicke Lewis, John Addington Symonds, and His Daughter Margaret Containing 22 Full-Page Illustrations Reproduced In The Colours Of The Originals 'The book will easily succeed in communicating to its readers the tonic crispness, and brightness of spirit which have been distilled into it from the highland sunshine and mountain air. - Scotsman.

Tyrol By E. Harrison Compton And W. A. Baillie-Grohman Containing 24 Full-Page Illustrations Reproduced In The Colours Of The Originals 'This striking and absorbing account of the attractions of the Tyrol and the Tyrolese.' - Standard.

The Upper Engadine By J. Hardwicke Lewis And Spencer C. Musson Containing 24 Full-Page Illustrations Reproduced In The Colours Of The Originals 'Altogether it is an artistic production, and will be a welcome addition to the libraries of all who know and love the district it describes.' - Birmingham Daily Post.

Published By A. & G. Black. Ltd., 4 Soho Square. London. W.

Other Beautiful Books On Flowers And Gardens - Each Containing Full-Page Illustrations In Colour Similar To Those In This Volume

Flowers And Gardens Of Japan

Flowers And Gardens Of Madeira

Gardens Of England

Kew Gardens

Dutch Bulbs And Gardens

The Garden That I Love

British Floral Decoration

A. And C. Black . Soho Square . London, W.

Agents

America - The Macmillan Company 64 & 66 Fifth Avenue, New York.

Australasia - Oxford University Press 305 Flinders Lane, Melbourne.

Canada - The Macmillan Company Of Canada, Ltd 27 Richmond Street West, Toronto.

India - Macmillan & Company, Ltd. Macmillan Building, Bombay
309 Bow Bazaar Street, Calcutta.

Lightning Source UK Ltd.
Milton Keynes UK
05 January 2010

148188UK00003B/3/P